Praise for

DRESS YOUR HOUSE
FOR SUCCESS

"This terrific new book should be required reading for every home seller. . . . It's filled with so many practical tips based on Webb's vast experience, a home seller can't help but succeed after studying it."

—ROBERT BRUSS, TRIBUNE MEDIA SERVICES,
San Francisco Examiner

"Martha Webb is a perfect example of how ordinary folks can figure out how to make their homes look great, and reap the benefits from it financially."

—ILYCE R. GLINK, REAL ESTATE MATTERS SYNDICATE,
Chicago Sun-Times

"Miss Webb's first four steps couldn't be simpler: Unclutter. Clean. Repair. Neutralize. . . . Then comes her secret weapon, Dynamizing™, or adding the small touches that make buyers start seeing your house as their home."

—VIRGINIA GREINER,
Washington Times

"A step-by-step program to help you create an appealing home."

—BARBARA HERTENSTEIN, HOME EDITOR,
St. Louis Post-Dispatch

Finding Home:

Buying the House That's Right for You

MARTHA WEBB

THREE RIVERS PRESS
NEW YORK

The practical information in this book is not a substitute for legal, financial, accounting, or other appropriate professional advice.

Some of the items described in this book, including the HomeFinders Kit, labels, and videos may be ordered directly from the author, at (800) 288-4635.

Published by Three Rivers Press, a division of Crown Publishers, Inc., 201 East 50th Street, New York, New York 10022. Member of the Crown Publishing Group.

Random House, Inc. New York, Toronto, London, Sydney, Auckland
www.randomhouse.com

THREE RIVERS PRESS and colophon are trademarks of Crown Publishers, Inc.

Printed in the United States of America

Design by Margaret Hinders

Library of Congress Cataloging-in-Publication Data
Webb, Martha.
    Finding home : buying the house that's *right* for you /
Martha Webb.
    1. House buying—United States.   2. Residential real estate—United
States—Purchasing.   3. Real estate business—United States.   I. Title.
HD255.W35   1998
643′.12—dc21   98-14306
                                                                     CIP

ISBN 0-609-80353-0

10 9 8 7 6 5 4 3 2 1

First Edition

For
Margie, Paula, David, Jason, and Whitney
David, Michael, and Sarah—
you are the magic of home.

And
In loving memory of Ben Clark,
who is missed every day.

Acknowledgments

There are seldom enough words or enough time to say thank you. Writing a book seems to take all the words and all the time. Committing my thanks to writing is forever and I am thankful for so many. This book is for the givers . . . and my heroes.

First, my mom, who has always shown me a better way and encouraged me to keep looking. Her example and her life have been an inspiration. And my father whose artistic talent was my gift.

My agent, Kim Witherspoon. She inspired me to look beyond . . . and through.

My editor, Pam Krauss, who encouraged this book from the beginning.

My friend Scott Stein. I am grateful for his friendship over the years. He gave graciously.

And my friend Lee Coats. His accolades mean so much.

No friend has been there more than Dave Coleman. His directing talents are only surpassed by his everyday support and celebration.

Barb Potter, who has stood beside me for hours and who overlooks my every fault.

Mike Rasmussen, a loyal employee and friend.

Barb and Jim Geiser, who embody the concept of neighbors.

My children. Margie, who inspires me to be like her. Paula, who brought my own words back to me when I needed them most, and so competently took over when all my time was taken. David, whose gentle ways and talents make me so proud. And my stepchildren, Jason and Whitney, who have brought so much joy to my life.

My brothers—my cheering section. Rick, whose confidence has been a guidepost. David, who challenges me to question.

Arthur Richenthal for his wise counsel and focus on the big picture. And, again, Joan Easton, who opened a door to yet another career.

Matt McKenzie, whose sense of design and humor has been an extraordinary addition to our group.

A special thanks to Greg Coenen, who at the last minute graciously and creatively added a new dimension to the book.

There isn't enough space in a dozen books to thank my clients and customers for their trust and confidence over the years.

And Bruce, who changed my life. His unconditional support leaves me in awe and it is here that words fail me.

I am blessed. And I am deeply grateful.

Contents

Introduction 11

1 *What Makes a House a Home?* 15

2 *Close Enough Isn't Good Enough* 24

3 *Step One: Designing Your HomePrint* 40

4 *Step Two: Assembling Your Resources* 73

5 *Step Three: Looking Through Walls* .96

6 *Step Four: The Art of the Deal* 119

7 This End up! *A Guide to Moving with More Fun
   and Less Hassle* 134

8 *Settling In* 165

Appendix I: *Property Information Sheet* 176

Appendix II: *Moving Materials* 184

Appendix III: *Words, Terms, and Real Estate* 186

Index 190

Introduction

Like most families, mine divides up the Sunday paper by our personal preferences: my husband takes the front section, my stepson grabs the sports page, and I beeline for the real estate section. I bought my first home thirty years and seventeen houses ago and I am always thinking about buying another. When I stop to think about it, I realize I've been fascinated with the concept of "home" since I was a child. At seventeen, when my parents moved us from our home of twelve years, I chose the house (admittedly within some carefully drawn parameters). Since my first apartment, I have moved sixteen times, finding home in five states and twelve different cities and suburbs. The moves have resulted from a gamut of life events: from a job transfer within days of the birth of a child to downsizing after a divorce. In the midst of all this change, the homes I have found have been havens and a source of comfort. Each has enhanced my life and my relationship with my family. Each has returned a sizable profit when it came time to sell.

I have always been equally fascinated with "streamlining"— searching for the most direct method to carry out a task, run an errand, even plant a garden. Whenever a task requires repetition, I set about creating an organized method to accomplish it more smoothly the next time. I'm frequently called a perfectionist, but I prefer to think of the characteristic as optimism. Optimism that there is always a clearer, more direct way. And in the search, my creativity has been challenged to design a method that results in a better solution. It is a trait that has resulted in multiple careers—

corporate administration, public relations and advertising, film production, and marketing consulting for Fortune 500 companies. I have consulted with companies undergoing corporate change and seeking to bring about cohesiveness. I have designed sales meetings and events to launch new products and new directions. I have stood before city councils outlining a better approach to development that would preserve a family neighborhood. My career has brought me in contact with a myriad of industries, from food manufacturing and health care, to sporting events promotion and even the "soda wars." Ultimately it has brought me home again.

Although I have never been a real estate agent, in 1989 I started my own company, BCW Video, to produce and distribute marketing products to the real estate industry—products that were designed to streamline the processes of buying and selling homes. It began with "Dress Your House for Success," a video to teach consumers my techniques for preparing a house to sell faster and at a higher price. The concept drew on my film production and communications background and, of course, my fascination with finding a better way. Since then, by applying my marketing techniques and following an organized step-by-step plan, hundreds of thousands of home sellers have reaped substantial financial benefits from the Dress Your House program.

I have continued to develop video products for the real estate industry and have been privileged to consult with both national and regional companies as well as individual sales associates, on how to help consumers discover the best way to sell a house and buy a house. In 1991, I introduced a similar tool for home*buyers*—a video to help them understand the homebuying process and a method for making their search more rewarding—financially and personally. When I conducted the first focus group, the unanimous response from veteran homebuyers was, "You gave me a whole new way to think about buying a house."

That new way to buy a *house* is to look at it as buying a *home*. It is based on the most fundamental of advertising and communication principles: communicating effectively depends on understanding your audience. It's the same when buying a house. To find a house that's right for your audience—your household—start by looking beyond the house. Start by looking at your lifestyle: *who* you are before *where* you are. When you look first at what activities comprise your lifestyle, you can more clearly define a location, house, and price range that support and enhance it. You'll be in control of all the change around you and emerge confident in your decisions and secure that you'll be making a sound financial investment.

Finding Home will help you integrate the emotional facet of home with the more tangible criteria: number of bedrooms, bathrooms, and size of mortgage. Isn't that what you're really searching for? After all, home is more about roots and family than it is about the structure of a house. It's about the magic of running through a door at the speed of childhood to share the day with someone you love or to seek the solace of a comfortable space. It's about a place that nurtures as well as protects. When we find a home and make a place for the ones we love, we are at the core of life. And nothing is more fulfilling than the warmth of family and friends in times of joy and in times of adversity. We start the search for a new home with the thrill and anticipation of finding just such a place. We know where we want to get, but the directions aren't always clear. Often the information available is at odds with the goal: investment opportunity, mortgage options, two bedrooms versus three or four. All important, but only part of the picture.

Finding Home is about the whole picture. My four-step program will give you a game plan and a context for all the elements. And it won't add any time to the process. In fact, *Finding Home* will *save* you time . . . and probably money, two precious commodities when you are making a purchase of this magnitude.

Organization is key in undertaking a multifaceted task. *Finding Home* will bring a new organization to your homebuying adventure. The HomePrint worksheets will help you organize and prioritize your criteria, which you'll balance with your financial objectives. You'll learn about a network of resources to draw from to make the process as uncomplicated as possible. And then, when the right house becomes your house, *Finding Home* shows you a straight road to your front door, complete with an orderly system for moving with less hassle and more time to bring the adventure full circle.

This book is for the buyer looking for a better way and clearer directions home.

CHAPTER 1

What Makes a House a Home?

When my husband and I decided to blend our two families, we knew it wouldn't be easy. In fact, I would have bet against us. Five children ranging in age from four to eighteen. Five tuitions and seven personal schedules.

We knew that the house we chose would play a key role in helping make this new family work. Mentally, we prepared a list. It had to have a bedroom for each child, and because our children attended three different schools, it had to be in a location convenient to each. We decided that water—a lake or a pool—would provide an atmosphere of fun and relaxation. And we wanted a house that could become a gathering place for teens and for extended family to help knit this group together. Both my husband and I work long hours and travel extensively; we wanted to be close to the office and the airport. And because we knew we'd move back to the city within ten years, once the kids were off on their own, resale potential was also critical.

Finally, a traffic pattern that fostered interaction was an important criterion on our househunting list because the floor plan of my previous house had proven disastrous for impromptu conversation with adolescents. Their bedrooms were tucked away at the end of a long hallway, providing privacy and isolation at the same time. The kitchen, originally designed for serving only, was isolated from the main living areas and the formal design of the living and dining rooms offered little incentive for "hanging out."

Given the number and diversity of our requirements, the search was exhausting and lengthy. We were determined to find what we wanted, and when timing began to get tight, we had to resist the temptation to "settle." We nearly bought two times because the house satisfied *most* of our criteria. When we finally decided on one, both my husband and I knew it wasn't quite the house of our dreams—we'd always envisioned us in a classical-style house near cultural activities and the excitement of the city—but it did have the potential to become the stuff of which dreams are made. It had all our top priorities: open floor plan, swimming pool, close to all three schools, and less than a half an hour drive from the office and the airport. Plus, it boasted a beautiful resortlike yard with a gazebo, trampoline, space that invited a wicked game of croquet, and the garden I didn't yet know I loved. The kitchen promised to foster my husband's gourmet excursions. Although it lacked the grace and warmth of a traditional style, the house's main areas had been expertly remodeled and updated—not to mention the fireplace, hot tub, and steam shower in the master suite!

That house was charmed. The floor plan worked, encouraging interaction that reduced stress and built friendships. The kitchen became the center of culinary adventures and casual conversations. I experienced the rewards of cultivating a garden. The yard and pool provided a setting for entertaining, from birthday parties to family reunions and holidays. I still can feel the warmth of watching my children, stepchildren, and their friends—often spanning an age range of ten years—deep in conversation while lounging on the trampoline. I cherish the memories of evenings in the gazebo talking and laughing with children and neighbors.

Although ours is a blended family, this house did indeed become our family home.

When four of our five children were later off on their own, we set out again to find a house to support a new lifestyle. The remarkably speedy sale of our house set the neighbors abuzz when, although it neither was the largest nor boasted the most amenities, it sold for substantially more than any house in the neighborhood ever had. We'd bought well and sold well. The house had given us eight wonderful years, hearts full of memories, and pockets full of cash to set off on another house adventure.

Was it luck? Maybe a little. But more than luck our story represents the benefits of focusing on finding the right house—one that is both a sound *life* investment and a sound *financial* investment.

If you're reading this book, you've probably already started scanning the Sunday real estate ads and made the decision to buy a house. You and millions of other Americans—over four million in fact—will buy a home and move this year. To many the story of our blended family house may sound like a fairy tale. After all, most of what is written about homebuying focuses on how to avoid the pitfalls or how to wade through the myriad details surrounding the purchase.

Our story is not a fairy tale; there is no magic to it. It's the result of a clearly defined process—making a plan and sticking to it. The key to finding the right house is knowing how to look for space that fits who you are and enhances your life, family, and work. My experience as a visual communicator has taught me to see beyond what is to what *can be*: to determine whether or not a space is supportive of my family and if it could enhance our lifestyle. You can learn the same skills.

After each of my sixteen moves, the first response from my family and friends has been: "This house is *you*! How did you find this place?" Although acquaintances consistently comment on how my houses are "me," the houses themselves have all been dramatically different. Each appeared to be me because it reflected a specific stage or situation of my life.

Taking the time to look back at where you've been, and to imagine realistically what your household will be like in the next five or more years, is the foundation for finding a home that works for *your* family—a space that can become a favorite place.

But there's more to a successful home purchase than finding a house that looks and feels great. A house you love may not automatically also be a sound financial investment. The average homeowner becomes a homeseller every five to eight years, and whether the moves are planned or result from unanticipated circumstances, the object is to build equity and accumulate wealth along the way. Because the real estate market is always in flux—interest rates rise and fall; neighborhoods gain or lose buyer appeal; and the numbers of available houses and buyers vary—there are no guarantees that your purchase will appreciate or that you'll be dancing on the way to the bank when it comes time to sell. Smart buyers, however, can hedge their bets. You can reasonably determine whether the house of your dreams will be a profitable investment.

Hedge your bets for the next sale.

The Three Stages of Buying

Every homebuying experience is different. It is unique to your individual circumstances and is further defined by the house you choose, the circumstances of the seller, the condition of the market, and the terms of the sale. However, all buyers move through three stages in buying a home. In some cases the stages are clearly recognizable and progress over a period of time ranging from several weeks to several years. In others the stages overlap and may appear to be one all-encompassing process occurring in a matter of days—or even hours. Regardless of your specific time frame and needs, by following the Finding Home plan you can take control of the process rather than find yourself at its mercy. Understanding the phases and doing thorough preparation will help you manage your decisions, your time, and your resources.

Stage 1, planning and defining, typically begins before looking at homes. You choose a location, the style and size of your next house, and your price range. The Game of Nines in Chapter 2 will bring a broader dimension to this stage and help you integrate lifestyle needs with subjective criteria on your HomePrint worksheets in Chapter 3. The suggestions in Chapter 4, "Assembling Your Resources," will ensure that when you venture out, sellers will perceive you as a desirable buyer.

Stage 2, the selection process and the time it takes, is determined by how thoroughly and accurately you've defined your needs and, of course, by the availability of houses that meet those needs. Average buyers look at a dozen or more houses over a period of six to eight weeks, beginning Stage 2 anew each time they approach a house for sale. The tour starts objectively. With your list in hand you immediately commence assessing—consciously or subconsciously—whether that property fits your criteria. If you're like many buyers you'll look for reasons *not* to buy as a way of eliminating choices. When you find features and amenities you like, you start to look more actively, searching for positive reinforcement. Chapter 5, "Looking Through Walls," will help you look beyond what is and imagine what can be. And the Househunters' Notes will provide an organized and efficient method of evaluating your options against your HomePrint.

Buy headfirst and heartfelt.

Progressing to the final stage, purchasing, happens when you feel an emotional connection to a particular house—when your heart says, "This is it . . . this is *home*." Your preparation will allow you to go headfirst with your heart's decision.

Although all buyers progress through the stages, they don't always do so with a plan—or even consciously. I have several clients and friends who seem to have just "found" themselves in the midst of the homebuying process. A few years ago a business associate with a demanding schedule attended a holiday party at the home of a colleague's girlfriend. Although he knew the couple well, it was the first time he'd been to her home. He arrived late to the party, and as he hurried up the front walk, he remarked about the beauty of the house. When he entered the foyer he was so taken with the home that he requested a tour. The first floor was exquisite, and, somewhat hesitantly, he asked if he could look upstairs. The host encouraged him to continue the tour, and he proceeded through the house—and the evening—in awe. As he left the party he jokingly told his friends that it really hadn't been fair to invite him—he was envious of the house and didn't relish the idea of returning to his own.

The next day he received a call from his colleague and instantly began expounding on how much he loved the house. Finally his colleague said, "Hold it! The reason I'm calling is to tell you we're getting married. If you love that house so much, why don't you buy it from her?" My associate responded in a heartbeat, "Let's talk about price." In a few short hours he had progressed directly through the first and second stages of homebuying. My associate hadn't really "known" he was looking for a house. But he realized that although he was a successful businessperson with a busy social life, at the end of the day he longed for the comforts of a cozy house in a quiet neighborhood. The "welcome home" feeling of this house, coupled with the relaxation of a holiday evening among friends, had caused those needs to surface. He *felt* at home. Then, although he knew the house was perfect for him, he proceeded as a businessperson, by stepping back and carefully assessing the location, style, price, and resale potential before negotiating the purchase.

Leaving the process to chance or proceeding without a plan—as many homebuyers do—doesn't always lead to a happy ending.

Four Steps to Homebuying Success

The objective of the Finding Home plan is to recognize a house that works on two levels: one that enhances households and strengthens relationships and one that builds equity and provides a return on your investment when the FOR SALE sign goes up. My four-step plan will show you how to determine where to look and how to evaluate what you see so the space you choose will add a new and positive dimension to your life. *Finding Home* will also show you how to calculate whether the home of your dreams could become a nightmare when it's time to sell. Make no mistake: buying a home is an emotional adventure. You may be tempted to skip a step, compromise, or set aside priorities when you see a house you love; that's to be expected. No house is perfect, and holding out for something that matches every minute specification will only cause frustration. However, if you do your homework and follow the steps outlined in Chapters 3 through 6, the compromises you choose will be made with the bigger picture in focus.

Focusing on the bigger picture gives you clearer directions home.

The Finding Home steps are easy to follow and can be tailored to fit your schedule. Step 1, Designing Your HomePrint, will focus your search and save you precious time. Step 2, Assembling Your Resources, will make certain you are *ready* to buy when an opportunity presents itself. Step 3, Househunting, will be organized and efficient, and when you are ready to purchase, you'll proceed confidently to Step 4, The Art of the Deal. You may want to jump right into the most fun element—househunting—but proceeding without a plan or a solid team of professionals can turn fun into stress and anxiety.

How much time will the Finding Home program add to the process of buying a house? None. You can complete the HomePrint worksheets in a morning; you can research locations in a day or two, and assemble your resources at the same time. In fact, *Finding Home* can actually *reduce* the time spent during the househunting phase and during the interval between finding a house and taking possession of it. Most important, *Finding Home* puts you in control of *when* your time is spent and the effect it has on your life. It's like having good directions to where you're going. When your directions are clear, you arrive relaxed and calm; when the journey is chaotic or fraught with wrong turns and backtracking, you often arrive frenzied and late. *Finding Home* is about the journey *and* the destination. When the journey is smooth, the destination is more rewarding.

Map out a straight road home.

Whether you're a first-time buyer looking for a starter home, a veteran making a move to accommodate a growing family, or a midlifer moving to launch a transition lifestyle at fifty, your goals are the same: to find a space that brings beauty and harmony to your life, a place where you'll be proud to entertain family and friends, and one that will nurture those you love. In fact, many repeat buyers have told me that this process has given them a whole new way to think about buying—a new sense of confidence that this move will be a real life adventure! So whether you've bought and sold a dozen homes or are just starting out, read this book through and do your homework before you start looking at houses. If your timetable is very tight, it may be necessary to overlap and blend some of the steps, but it's important to observe each one. The benefits of doing so will be both tangible and intangible. You'll increase the chance that this buy will result in an enhanced lifestyle now and a profitable sale down the road.

So grab a pencil and make yourself comfortable. Chapter 2 will get you started laying the foundation for finding home.

Close Enough
Isn't Good Enough

The birth of a child leaves little room in your life for anything else. In fact, nothing other than taking care of this new-
born and your family seems to matter. Life is a blur, a combination
of excitement and fatigue. The last thing you need is a job transfer.

My second child was ten days old when the news came. I don't
remember exactly how I felt, or if I could even understand the sig-
nificance of the event in the midst of caring for a two-year-old and
an infant who didn't sleep at night! Although the transfer had been
anticipated throughout a yearlong training period, and my husband
and I were eager to establish roots in a town that we hoped would
be home for many years, the timing couldn't have been worse. Finding a house—what should have been a thrilling adventure—was
just a small piece in a bigger picture filled with the excitement of a
promotion, the anxiety of moving farther from relatives, and the
responsibilities of caring for a growing family.

We decided to look for a larger house, with at least three bedrooms, and my husband went ahead to start his new job and find
the new house. Coordinating the move was overwhelming, and I
just assumed we'd find a house as charming as our last—a small
two-bedroom cottage on a lake. However, our new town had a pop-

ulation of just 30,000, and the housing market wasn't exactly booming. We didn't like any of the three-bedrooms available in our price range. Because we'd gone the route of living in a motel with one small child while looking for our previous house, we knew firsthand the stress of confinement, and living in such close quarters with two children was out of the question. So when my husband found a two-bedroom town house, we decided to settle rather than wait for a house that fit our criteria. True, it was smaller than we'd hoped, but my husband assured me the other amenities compensated for the size—it was new, with a large kitchen and the hardwood floors I'd wanted.

Despite these assurances, my heart sank when I walked in the door. The kitchen was large, but there was no dining room. I directed the movers to take my dining room set and prized antique china cabinet directly to the basement. Our unit faced north and had little natural light. Although the second bedroom was larger than the bedroom in the cottage, it seemed cramped with both a crib and a youth bed. And because the unit was new, it didn't *feel* as cozy as the less spacious cottage had. My two-year-old daughter, who had loved the freedom of lakeside living—hours of throwing rocks from the bridge and searching for spring flowers in the nearby woods— was suddenly confined by a more urban lifestyle. Having to share my time and her room with a sister who awakened her several times a night created a very cranky toddler. The restrictive schedule of an infant compounded my own feeling of isolation in a new town, where I had few acquaintances.

After six months we decided we had to make a move. There was now an ample supply of larger houses on the market in our price range, and we found a three-bedroom home in a great family neighborhood. It was full of charm and had large bedrooms, a sunroom with space for adults and kids to relax and play, and, of course, a dining room that could hold the furniture we had put in storage.

The house needed decorating, but we'd gotten a terrific buy, and I was thrilled with the potential. We carefully planned the projects to be undertaken and knew this home would give us years of pleasure. The house made a marked improvement in our family interaction and lifestyle, but, of course, our corporate relocation program didn't provide assistance for rectifying a shortsighted move, and the financial burden was ours.

By allowing the changes in our life to overshadow the importance of the home we selected, we put ourselves in a situation where the house itself became a problem. Had we held true to our criteria, the transition time of a new family and new job would have been more manageable. I could have stayed in our previous house with the children until a house in our new town became available, or we could have stored our belongings and rented a larger, furnished space, avoiding the financial burden of a second move. Ah, hindsight.

America is on the move. On the first of every month grocery stores are hounded for boxes, truck and trailer rentals skyrocket, and the streets are crowded with moving vans. In addition to the millions of homeowners who will buy homes and move this year, countless more will move to and from rentals. The cycle usually begins with moving from your family home in your late teens or early twenties. You're off to college or a first apartment, and it seldom takes more than a few carloads to move your belongings. Buying a house is probably the last thing you're thinking about at this time; however, even these first moves set your perception of the process. For most adults just the word *moving* can cause shivers. It brings images of hours and days spent packing, heavy boxes and appliances to be carried, and the disarray of the first weeks in a new space. We've all thought to ourselves: I'm never

> Changes bring moves; moves bring change.

moving again. They'll have to carry me out of here feet first. I've said it a dozen times.

The Moving Cycle

However, few people move to one house and stay put these days. The moving cycle—looking and buying, physically moving, settling in and making home, and finally selling and beginning the process again—will be repeated sporadically through one's lifetime. At times it may be unpredictable; at other times it will be more calculated. While some moves will be in conjunction with the joys of life—marriage, new and expanding families, career advances—others will result from less happy circumstances—divorce, job loss, or change in health.

Frequently, the circumstances surrounding a move will involve powerful life-changing events that can overshadow the process of finding home. The magnitude of these events, planned or unplanned, demands so much time and energy that finding a home becomes just one of many details on a long list of things to do. It's no wonder that many of us choose space that is "good enough" at the time but, when the dust has settled, is less than we'd hoped for. When moving accompanies a major life event, having a clearly delineated process to follow helps avoid shortsighted decisions. It becomes a safety net to ensure you don't overlook the details or too readily reprioritize your needs just to ease the stress.

When the dust settles, will you be at home?

Millions of homeowners choose to buy a new home to accommodate their growing families or to reflect a change in their lifestyle or earning power. Most people move every five to eight years during the prime earning and family-rearing years. Jobs change and incomes rise. In a few short years a grade-schooler grows enough to take up the space of an adult, or a house once filled with the activity of a family becomes a stopping point during college vacations. Neighborhood demographics change as each household goes through its own life cycle—a once quiet street becomes filled with skateboards and bicycles as retirees move out and young families move in. A recent survey of eighteen major U.S. markets reported that "move-up" buyers accounted for more than 55 percent of home sales. In many of these situations the moving "process" goes on for years. For example, my good friends spent eight years in their first house. For several years, as their incomes and their children grew, they talked of moving to a larger home and better school district. They looked at houses off and on. When their youngest child was about to enter middle school, they decided the time was finally right. No other event *prompted* the move, but the move *reflected* a desired change in lifestyle and therefore required an assessment of how a new house and location could support an upwardly mobile family direction over the next five to eight years, before the children left home.

Without the financial burden of family demands, a growing segment of over-fifty buyers are defying the notion that they should scale back and are opting to move to or build the house they always wanted. Turning fifty—as more than 10,000 baby boomers do *each day*—is becoming a launching point for new careers *and* new homes. However, many in this group have been out of the home-buying market longer than younger, more mobile homeowners. While they may have bought and sold several homes over the course of their lives, the process has changed dramatically: the paperwork alone has increased an estimated 35 percent. For these buyers, purchasing a house may entail greater risks than for homebuyers with more moves down the road—and more opportunities to rectify a shortsighted decision.

The 1997 federal tax law broadened the options for all home-owners. Before the changes homeowners were allowed only one tax-free exemption from capital gains when selling a house, and the move had to occur after age fifty-five. With those limitations lifted most homeowners can move from high-cost to low-cost markets, reap the benefits of home improvements or a suddenly desirable location, or downsize without penalties. Over forty million baby boomers in their forties and fifties now have more options for *right*sizing to suit a lifestyle without children at home.

New laws mean new avenues for *life*sizing.

Several years ago I helped a retiree with a home purchase. She'd enjoyed renting a fabulous condominium space—two large bedrooms, a charming dining room, and a kitchen with the latest appliances and cabinetwork. When the owner sold the property, she was forced to move before finding a new home. She had been storing her furniture and renting a smaller apartment for several months, and was anxious to get resettled. We searched condominiums and town houses, but nothing compared with the space she'd had. When we finally found a town home with the same grace and style, plus a guest bedroom for grandchildren and a cozy living room and fireplace, she made an offer, only to lose it to another bidder.

Knowing how difficult it had been to find such a space, and feeling concerned about taking a down payment from her retirement funds, she opted to rent a condo. It was a perfect building, but the rent on a two-bedroom unit was a little more than she had budgeted, so she chose a one-bedroom. The rent has since risen and now exceeds what her mortgage payments would have been. The space is lovely, but there is no room for grandchildren to spend the night, and it is barely large enough to accommodate the entertaining that had been a big part of her life. Moving again is a dreaded thought, so she continues to get by with space that's nice but just short of fulfilling her real lifestyle needs. Perhaps a better solution would have been found had she met with her tax accountant to evaluate financial alternatives and waited for another town home to come on the market that fit her budget *and* her lifestyle.

Close Enough Is Another Term for Settling

Certainly not every home purchase can be easily classified as a good buy or a bad one. Homebuying involves compromises, and you will likely find yourself weighing the benefits of two or more houses. However, there are situations when you are most likely to settle for "close enough." A client who has worked with the corporate relocation market for over a decade, helping CEOs and new hires alike find houses, describes the two most common situations in which homeowners are likely to settle for other than what they really want or need.

The first settling situation occurs when frustration sets in—from either losing out on a house you love or not immediately finding one that meets your criteria. You purchase the next house you see for fear of losing it or never finding what you want. My retiree client is a classic example of this situation. After holding out for the right house and then losing it, she settled.

Losing a house—or your heart—can cloud your vision.

The other situation may not appear on the surface to be settling. It occurs when homebuyers make a decision strictly on emotion. They lose their hearts to a home and get tunnel vision. They either don't bother to evaluate the house thoroughly as a financial investment or are so enthralled with certain features that they overlook—

consciously or unconsciously—whether the house is actually a good fit for their household and their financial situation.

Several houses ago my house seemed to be growing smaller as my children grew taller. My family and my taste in decorating had outgrown the space we were in. I was finding myself looking longingly at larger houses and casually reading the Sunday real estate ads. Late one afternoon I found an ad for a house that sounded just perfect: four bedrooms (one more than we had), large dining room (I was feeling cramped when entertaining family and friends), in a desirable location where my children wouldn't have to change schools, and at a bargain price. I excitedly showed the ad to my children, and although we had missed the open house, we piled into the car to take a look. It was my dream house. A beautiful New England colonial with a picket fence, a full two stories that promised elbowroom for growing teens. And it was within a few blocks of a lake for walking and jogging.

We called the real estate agent and arranged an immediate showing. When we walked in I *knew* this was the home of my dreams. It oozed elegance. The curved staircase conjured fairy-tale images of family life in this house. Each room had character, and although the upstairs was dated, it was not in need of structural work, and I felt it would be a delight to decorate these charming spaces. I was so taken with the home and happy that it met my list of wants and needs (not to mention the great price), it never occurred to me this might not be the perfect home for my family.

For the first year I was busy decorating and planning. I contracted for bathroom updating. I set about transforming the upstairs to show off the nooks and crannies, window seats and interesting spaces.

Within a year I knew something was wrong. The house just didn't feel right. Although it was in the same school district as our former home, the children's friends were too far away for spontaneous get-togethers, and the kids spent much of their free time in the rec room. I felt estranged from them, a fact I attributed at the time to their teenage years. The bathroom projects were more extensive than I had anticipated, and it felt like the entire house was torn apart. The house needed more work than I had time. The mortgage payments were stretching my budget, and the neighborhood was not as friendly as the one we'd left. I soon dreaded pulling into the driveway. It became apparent that instead of supporting my family's needs, the house, by its formal layout, design, and location, was actually pulling us apart. The most frequently used entrance, a side

The wrong house can wreak havoc on your life.

door, was within a few steps of a basement recreation room and tempted teens to go directly downstairs, remaining out of earshot and sight. (My children laugh at this story now, telling me it was a *great* house because I had no idea what they were doing—my point exactly!) The house felt lonely, and although I knew my family was changing, I also knew that the house itself was contributing to my negative feelings. Remodeling was neither an option for my tight budget nor a wise investment because the result would have placed the home in the upper price range of the neighborhood.

I accelerated the bathroom projects and put the house back on the market just eighteen months after we'd moved in. Because it was in a high-demand location and I'd improved it wisely—keeping the price at the median of the neighborhood—I realized a substantial profit. But it wasn't worth the emotional price I'd paid.

You may find a beautiful home in a highly desirable neighborhood, but if it doesn't work for your family, it's still a bad investment. If I'd kept my eye on the bigger picture, I'd have made a different choice.

The Game of Nines

So how do you avoid these mistakes? How can you see clearly enough to evaluate if your next house will be the *right* house? It begins with looking back. The best place to start is looking at what works for you now and what has worked in the past. What do you love about your current house or another place you've lived? It's tempting to leapfrog this question because we seldom move when we've already found the ideal situation. The root of a move is change, so the tendency is to look forward rather than back. Many real estate agents and homebuying books start with the question "What is your dream home?" This is usually followed with questions designed to arrive at how much house you can afford. Those questions are important, and we'll get to them. But first and foremost, finding a *home* is about establishing roots, and roots are strengthened by building on the past. Deciding on a location and a house for the future can be a clearer process if you look at what strengthened your household in the past.

Hindsight gives you insight.

Begin with an exercise I call the Game of Nines. The goal is to focus on what's important to each member of your household. Looking at *who* you are before determining *where* you are will provide the foundation for creating your personal HomePrint—a blueprint of the house that best complements your household's needs and financial goals. Gather everyone over snacks, or head to your favorite restaurant with a notebook and an hour to spare.

Start by compiling two lists: nine favorite things about your house and location, and nine things you really don't care for. There are no right or wrong answers, and everyone's likes and dislikes are valid. Include features, activities, favorite spaces, and neighborhood attributes. If you find yourself with a list longer than nine, that's fine.

The importance of the exercise is to look broadly at your life and how it interacts with your house. You may find yourself starting to define what type of house you want your next home to be. If so, make notes and set them aside to enter on your HomePrint worksheets in Chapter 3.

When I was forty-eight my husband and I made a lifestyle move. As perfect as our house had been for our family, it had never been *our* dream house. We both love older homes and the activity of a city setting. However, with a blended family that included four teenagers and a preschooler, such a location was out of the question. So we put the dream on hold.

Eight years later, in a household of three instead of seven, we began to live differently. Months would pass without my going into the upstairs bedrooms; more time was spent away from home; tending the yard that was so perfect for family gatherings wasn't a welcome chore when I'd rather spend an afternoon at a museum or extend a business trip through the weekend. The pool, a draw for teens and family, was requiring more maintenance because it was receiving so little use, and the expense became harder and harder to justify. When it sprang a leak and the pump needed replacing, I thought of dozens of ways I'd rather spend $2,000. Ultimately, we became dissatisfied spending time, money, and energy to maintain a house that wasn't supporting our current lifestyle, and we began to talk about moving.

Paint a picture of what you need to live the way you want.

My husband, stepson, and I spent a Saturday lunch refining our Game of Nines, and it became clear that the features and activities we loved about our first house together were no longer as important. Next, we carefully evaluated the financial consequences of a move. This took place before the capital gains tax change, so we calculated whether it would be more beneficial to stay in our home

Nine Things We Love About Our House Now	Nine Things We Don't
Deck	Long freeway drive to work
Gazebo—talking at night & entertaining	Contemporary design
	Lack of formal dining room
Trampoline	
Neighbors	No wood floors or trim
Kitchen—space for cooking & conversation	No "nooks and crannies"/ character
Mature landscaping; gardening	Too far from theater
	Lack of interesting outdoor walking areas
Windows across the back that bring in the outdoors and the light	Small kids' bedrooms—no space for sleepovers
Privacy of kids' room and bath	Lack of diversity in suburb
Office/den combination	

until age fifty-five, downsize, and move to a city out of the snow belt or to move now and move again in ten years. Nearly every answer pointed to moving now to a home and lifestyle better suited for our half-empty nest. Our initial decisions were calculated and weighed, and they helped us clearly define *where* to look and *what* houses to look at. The result has been an exhilarating and satisfying experience. Our new house has been as rewarding as the last house. The process we followed and the success it yielded became the genesis of the Finding Home program.

Our hundred-year-old home, in the heart of the city, is near museums, lakes, restaurants, unique retail shops, and theaters. While the square footage is nearly identical to that of our suburban home, the houses are dramatically different, reflecting our life and work styles: three compact stories with main living areas, including an office, on the first floor; a second-floor "suite" with two baths, master and guest bedrooms, plus a sunporch/exercise room; and a third-floor haven for a teenager: bedroom, study, bath, and deck. The beautifully landscaped yard takes just ten minutes to mow and boasts charming spaces to plant—or not plant—the flowers I love.

This move was rooted in adventure and a new sense of freedom. It has given me more flexibility than I have ever known. And as much as I love my new house, I love my new life. It added a new dimension to our relationship. We're as free as twenty-year-olds making a first move, but with a lot more money. I'm able to decorate without making concessions to children's activities or other budget priorities. The reduced maintenance requirements mean more time for travel and a more flexible workstyle. And what's more, we were able to make the move without adverse financial repercussions. On page 35 you can see what we included in our last Game of Nines.

The message of home greets you every day.

Pay attention to the more subtle things that make your home feel warm and inviting, like the way sunlight lights up the porch in the afternoon, or dapples through the bedroom in the early morning. Include activities that are facilitated by the house or its location, such as a pool or a nearby lake or walking trail. Think of the feeling of coming home

Does Your Household Include Children?

Involving children early on in the moving process will play an important role in helping them adjust to a new environment. Here are some suggestions to ease the transition:

- Include children in your Game of Nines.
- Initiate family meetings and discuss concerns openly and honestly to build harmony and soothe anxieties.
- Start one or more of the projects on page 149. Or, if your move schedule is tight, purchase a disposable camera and help your child take pictures to be developed after the move.
- When you've settled on a house, create a positive sense of anticipation. Explore your new neighborhood. Find activities and places of interest to everyone.
- Take your children to visit their new school. If you're moving to a new city, ask the principal to send information before the move. For younger children, ask for letters from their new teachers.
- Help each child pack his or her room or a box of favorite things to be opened first. Packing can be a therapeutic method of letting go, and favorite items will provide comfort in new places.
- Be a role model. If you display a positive attitude about the move, your children will emulate it. You may find that it will improve *your* outlook, too!

after a long day at work, a business trip, or a vacation. What is it about your house that says "Welcome home"? When I approach my current house, the sight of people walking, jogging, and biking around the lake is a signal of the relaxation that comes from both the exercise I love and a closeness to nature in the midst of the city. As I come up the front walk, the brick patio and rocking chairs greet me with recollections of entertaining family and friends. Those feelings translate into two favorite features: outdoor exercise space and outdoor entertaining space.

After our recent move we decided to help my stepson adapt to city life by exploring the neighborhood on foot. Having spent most of his twelve years in a commuting suburb, he found this intriguing and interesting. The idea expanded to walking to breakfast on weekends, and we have continued to walk to restaurants and theater. Close proximity to our favorite activities will definitely make our list of favorites in our next Game of Nines.

If you're a first-time homebuyer, look at what you loved about your family home, or a friend's house. What features of those houses did you find appealing, and what activities and hobbies did they support? Buyers whose move is a part of a life change, such as marriage, relocation, retirement, or divorce, will need to give more thought to this exercise to make certain it isn't overshadowed by current circumstances. When I moved after a divorce, it was difficult to think positively about the change. Taking the time to do this exercise helped me look at how simulating certain past features and activities could make for a smoother transition.

Next, talk about the things you don't really like. This is often more difficult than listing the things you love because while living in a house you tend to overlook its faults. You pay little attention to the things you don't actually like because they are usually intertwined with the more pleasant aspects of home. For example, if you are inclined to include "big yard" on the list of things you don't like, be more specific. Is it the yard, or do you dislike mowing the lawn or weeding a garden? Give some thought also to the activities you forgo because of location or lack of specific features in your house. Perhaps you don't pursue a hobby you love because you don't have space to work, or you easily

> What you *don't* like is as meaningful as what you *do* like.

sidestep exercise because the health club or walking trails are too far away.

Once you have your two lists, look to see what may be in conflict. For example, when our family talked about our big yard, we all agreed it involved too much work, and we listed it on the "Don't" side. But gardening was on my list of things I *loved*. If you really dislike specific characteristics, such as uneven floors or constantly cracking walls, but love the warmth of the woodwork in your older home, you may find a compromise is in order when defining what type or age of home to look at. Refer to your Game of Nines as you make your HomePrint.

Your Game of Nines will be as diverse as your household and is guaranteed to bring up stories of times tucked away. Reflecting will elicit laughter and perhaps some sadness. But the exercise will expand your thinking and translate into concrete definitions in the next chapter. With your Game of Nines in hand, you're ready to design your own HomePrint, a plan to follow to keep your eye on the bigger picture. When you've completed a long day of house-hunting, you'll be able to compare your notes and objectively evaluate whether the houses you've seen are potentially sound investments that fit your lifestyle and your financial goals. You'll define the locations and physical house layout that are best suited for your household. And you'll add a price range to the formula to further focus your search.

CHAPTER 3

Step One:
Designing Your HomePrint

My daughter is about to become a first-time homebuyer. She's among the group that is changing the statistical norms for homeowners. She's single, female, and under thirty. When she finally made the decision to buy, excitement set in. She established a broad price range and identified several neighborhoods that seemed both fitting for a young professional and, she presumed, held high resale potential. She pored over the newspaper, searched the Internet, and charted an open house itinerary. Good idea, I thought. Go out and see what houses cost and what's available.

I wasn't surprised when she found several houses she liked and wanted me to look at two favorites. One was a quaint, small, newly remodeled home in a family neighborhood just outside the city. The other was larger, had been architect remodeled, and was in the heart of a thriving area of urban activity. She favored the larger home, which was slightly out of her price range but still feasible with a larger down payment.

She contacted her agent to look at the house with us. When we arrived the owner, who was selling on his own, told us they had accepted an offer pending receipt within two days of a letter from the buyer's mortgage company. I watched my daughter's heart sink and sensed her resolve. Since she'd first looked at the property, she had begun to imagine living in it and was convinced it was worth depleting her savings for this house. Fear of losing the house set in, and before I knew it she'd asked her agent to prepare an offer in case the buyer's approval letter wasn't received by the seller's deadline. When the seller confirmed receipt of the letter, my daughter was somewhat relieved because of the high down payment that would have been required, but she was disappointed over losing the house. The smaller house was still available and was now much more attractive because of the lower price. She was certain that losing the larger house was meant to be and wanted to make an offer on the smaller house before it sold, too.

As fate would have it, I had an opportunity to watch a demonstration of a software program that allows real estate professionals to show buyers a "snapshot" of a neighborhood, including pricing and selling trends, demographics, school facts, and crime statistics. I decided to test the software with the address of the house my daughter wanted to buy. The reports were sobering: this charming home was already priced in the upper tier of the neighborhood, and the selling trend in the past six months had seen nearly a 15 percent decrease, making it unlikely to return her investment. In addition, the owner-to-rental ratio was 35:65, indicating a move away from a strong family neighborhood.

With this comprehensive picture, the house quickly lost its appeal. My daughter decided it was time to step back, start from the beginning, and find a house that she loved *and* that would be likely to return her investment. She is now much more analytical in her search. Last I checked, that house was still for sale.

One essential aspect of successful homebuying is keeping the whole picture in view throughout the process. To do that you'll need to define objectively three key criteria—location, type of house, and price range. These criteria compose your HomePrint and start to paint a picture of your next house: where you want it to be, how you envision it will look and feel, and how you want it to affect your financial situation. As you answer these questions, it will become clear that all three components are interrelated. For example, based on *how much* you want to spend, what *size* house you need will determine *where* you can look. By the same token, *where* you want to live and *how much* you want to spend may determine what *size* house you can buy.

Prioritizing your responses will keep you focused when the choices are many. Your HomePrint will provide a realistic view of the house you're searching for and enable you to keep your head while losing your heart to a curved staircase or leaded glass china cabinets. You'll be better able to see beyond a seller's furnishings and decorating styles to evaluate and imagine how it would feel to come home to this house. Then, when the house that captures your heart measures up as a sound real estate investment, you'll feel a sense of confidence and security—that you've thoroughly weighed every aspect of this major decision and your choice is a sound life investment *and* financial investment.

As you read through this chapter, discuss the choices with your family and complete the worksheets that follow each section: "Defining Location," "Determining What Type of House Will Make the Best Home," and "Estimating Your Buying Power." You may want to ask each person in your household to complete the first two worksheets alone and then compare the results. Are your priorities consistent? Is your dream of living on a lake *your* dream, or is it shared? Are there concerns or fears to consider? Taking time during this pre-househunting phase to talk about your answers, discuss the differences, and reach some compromises

------ 🏠 ------

Common objectives avert wrong turns.

will avoid stress down the road. Refer to your Game of Nines to see what may be in conflict with your lifestyle. For example, when we talked about the work a pool and big yard entailed, the pendulum swung too far. We said, "Let's move to a condo!" But gardening and outdoor entertaining were on the list of things we love, so we knew a condo wasn't the solution.

I. Defining Location

Your HomePrint begins with the most important consideration in purchasing a house—location. Location is the only element of your house you can't change. It will be one of the most important marketing factors when it comes time to sell. And, though it may seem a remote possibility to you now, I can almost guarantee that you *will* sell at some point down the road. You'll forget the hassle of the move (or you'll follow the moving program in Chapter 7 and realize it doesn't have to be a nightmare) and decide to move to a bigger or smaller house, or some life event will come along and you won't have much choice. When you join the homebuying ranks again, you will start the process by selling your house. You'll wonder how quickly it will sell and for how much. The answer most always will be determined by location, condition, and price. You can change and control condition and price but not location. So the best time to think about selling is when you're buying.

A good location
is your ace
in the hole.

A good location will almost always give you an edge in the real estate market. While the appeal of a certain neighborhood can change over the years, it is less likely to fluctuate as often or as drastically as other market factors that influence selling prices: interest rates, number of homes available, and the number of buyers in the market. Location has been a key reason my houses have been profitable investments. The houses may not always have been ideally suited for my household, but each has sold quickly and profitably because location has always been my first consideration when buying.

The location of a house has two facets: the macroview, a municipality or section of a city; and the microview, a specific neighborhood within that town or area, or even the location of a house within a neighborhood. In the HomePrint stage, you'll be looking at the *macro*view of location. Keep in mind that any city has several "best" locations, generally characterized by appreciating home values, good schools, low crime rate, proximity to shopping, recreation, entertainment, and transportation. All these factors combine to determine resale potential, in terms of both the time it will likely take to sell and the return you can expect on your investment.

During our long search for our blended family house, we looked at one we now call "the house in the woods." It was in a highly desirable suburb and near one of the schools that two of our children attended. On a gravel drive more than a mile from the main road, the striking contemporary structure was surrounded by woods as if it had been lowered onto its foundation without disturbing a single tree. A gently flowing creek wound through the property, and the house captured our vision of a distinctive family home. It had been built by an architect, and every detail was designed to integrate the house with its surroundings, like a child's bedroom with built-in, angled bunks that felt like a treehouse, and a kitchen/great room that looked out over the creek and incorporated natural wood and fibers.

We fell in love with the house, the comfort and quiet of the property and tried to find reasons to justify purchasing it. It was located in a great suburb—but on the far western end and nearly an hour from the city. The price was great—but it had been reduced several times, probably reflecting that few buyers wanted to live that far out, in both distance and design. We still thought long and hard. We revisited the house several times before we could let it go, understanding it would probably be on the market as long *next* time as it had been *this* time. If you have to decide between the house of your dreams in a hard-to-sell area or style and a house with some compromises in a great location with high resale potential, the choice is clear.

In your Game of Nines you clarified the aspects of your lifestyle that will help reveal which locations can support who you are and what you *love* to do. For example, we are art and restaurant lovers, and will always find time to venture to a museum opening, catch a movie, or relax at a restaurant after a long day at work. The house in the woods wouldn't have provided much flexibility for that side of who we are. Do you have hobbies or consistent social activities that occur in one area more than others? Look at your life now and five years out. What aspects of your current lifestyle will you want to continue, and what new elements might you want to incorporate? How will your priorities or household change? Will your household grow, do you need day care, or will your children be going off to school? Will you have aging parents to consider? How long do you plan to live in this house?

Evaluate your working style now and in the future. When the demands on our time shifted from parenting several children to only one, we felt more freedom to tailor our workstyle. For example, my husband prefers to work both at home and in his office, often in the same day. I like to stay at home until midmorning and work later in the evening. Being close to our office makes our styles of working easy to accommodate.

Choosing a location will be easier if you know the city than if you're new to the area. However, the same principles apply to both

> If you opt for a high-risk choice, be aware of the long-term impact.

situations. You'll re-evaluate the specific neighborhood again before you make an offer on a house, but carefully researching the general location can save time by focusing the search and having your homework done. You may ultimately make some concessions for a special location or a unique house, but you'll do so with your eyes open if you check it out now.

There are some tried-and-true methods for sizing up a locale:

- Grade the public schools. Schools are an excellent qualifier when deciding on a location. Even if your household doesn't include school-age children, good school districts generally indicate good resale potential. If schools are a concern and you are relocating from another city, spend a day talking with principals of several schools before deciding where to look for a house. Statistics such as student-teacher ratio, expenditure per pupil, and test rankings will help you make an informed decision. Within each school look at the curriculum, special programs, and activities that are important to your family. My brother has a budding hockey star in his family. His criteria for buying a house definitely reflected each school's hockey program and its opportunities for his son.

  ---— 🏠 ———

  Scouting a location can reveal treasures—or traps.

- Go to city hall. Check plans for zoning changes or construction. Research employment statistics, average selling prices, trends in pricing, and owner-to-rental ratios.

- If your household uses public transportation, check the schedules and any planned changes and improvements.

- Read neighborhood newspapers and attend community meetings. This can provide insight into the workings of a location. What issues are important to the residents? What emphasis is placed on the activities that are important to you?

● Talk with the police department about crime statistics. Is there an increase or decrease? What are the most prevalent offenses?

If you're beginning to think, Whoa, this is a lot of work, and starting to question whether you have the time to be thorough, you might want to consider choosing a real estate agent now rather than later. (See "Choosing a Real Estate Agent," page 80.) An agent will have quick access to much of the statistical information to help you hone in on locations that suit your household's lifestyle and financial goals. If you are relocating to another city or state, the *Places Rated Almanac* (Macmillan), available at the public library, provides broad information about all 351 official metropolitan areas in the United States and Canada. It includes rankings and profiles on education, crime, employment, arts, and more. It isn't a substitute for specific neighborhood statistics, but it will provide a picture of the overall quality of life.

Relying solely on location recommendations from co-workers or other acquaintances can be risky. Their recommendations are likely to be based on personal likes and dislikes and may not reflect complete knowledge of an area. There is also a natural tendency to want people to think their community or neighborhood is a good place to live. I've never had friends tell me *not* to consider their neighborhood. Remember, nothing can replace statistics as an aid to an informed decision.

———— ● ————

Investigate community plans for resale hazards.

A client who works with corporate transferees recently designed an itinerary for a couple who were visiting our city to house-hunt before their impending transfer. He selected several houses in their price range and in locations that fit their criteria. He specifically omitted one house that was next to a proposed high-traffic road,

Preapprove Your Neighborhood

The most valuable advice you'll receive is to buy a neighborhood before you buy a house. Use this checklist to make certain you've thoroughly researched your target location:

- Evaluate the real estate environment: What is the average selling price of a house and length of time on the market? What is the median home value? What are the pricing trends over the past year? What is the owner-to-rental ratio? How many FOR SALE signs do you see? Are the houses well maintained? What do the cars look like?

- Think about the community: How do the demographics match your expectations? What are the median age and median household income?

- Review the school statistics: Check student-teacher ratios, expenditures per pupil, graduation rates, and test rankings. Ask about special enrichment programs, extracurricular and summer activities. Meet with principals and members of parent organizations. Ask about transportation services.

- Assess community services: Find out about street maintenance and waste removal. What type of community recreation is available? Talk with the police department about crime statistics: How do they compare with those of other areas, and what is the trend?

- What public transportation is available?

- Listen to the environment: How close are major highways? Do you hear airplanes or other traffic noises?

- Visit city hall and inquire about planned zoning changes and construction. Where are industrial sites? Are any hazardous waste sites nearby?

- Visit a coffee shop, library, or park. Are you comfortable? Are retail shops thriving and well kept? Stop and talk to local residents.
- Pick up a community newspaper and look at the concerns and issues and how the local government responds.

knowing that the resale potential would be questionable. After several unproductive tours the couple went back to their hotel for a dinner engagement with future co-workers. The next day they called to report they'd found a great house through these people. Sure enough, the house they'd found was the one the agent had omitted from the tour. The co-workers' suggestions were based on limited knowledge of the neighborhood.

When you've narrowed your choice of locations, take a drive through several neighborhoods. A driving tour is a great way to get an overview of the market and validate your expectations. Don't look at specific houses yet; look at the area. Make note of what you like and don't like. Are your expectations of the area realistic? Do the houses look like you pictured them? What are the traffic patterns? Is there noise from major highways, or is it in a flight path? Is there an excessive number of FOR SALE signs? Get out and walk around, or stop in the local coffee shop and talk to residents. Retail shops will reveal much about the area. Are they thriving? What is the condition of the storefronts and shopping centers? Are there many vacancies?

After I published my first book, *Dress Your House for Success,* which shows homesellers how to package their properties for a fast and profitable sale, I was asked by a television station to demonstrate the principles. Several agents had listings they felt could benefit from the concept and were eager to have me select their clients' houses. The house that caught my attention was in a high-demand family suburb and had been on the market for more than six months without an offer. The agent described the home as generally clean but in need of "warming up." It sounded like a perfect candidate for my Dynamizing™ technique, which creates impressions through-

out a house that cause buyers—or anyone—to *feel* at home.

🏠

Even a house in great condition won't compensate for a poor location.

When I arrived to look at the house, I was surprised it hadn't sold. The neighborhood was exceptionally well kept—a picture of suburban family living. The house's exterior was attractive and as inviting as any I'd seen.

But when I walked in I knew exactly why the agent had called: the house felt uninviting because it was so stark. It was an easy problem to fix. Borrowed furniture, artwork, and the addition of plants and linens quickly transformed the house into a picturesque home for a young family.

What I hadn't been told about, and what I couldn't fix, was the location. The backyard bordered a busy road. Before I was called in, the owners had finished a lower level to increase the usable square footage and the house's appeal. Their money would have been better spent on a fence and a wall of trees!

After Dynamizing™, the house sold, but not without a major price reduction to compensate for the poor location.

Remember, when it comes time to sell, you can dress your house for success and price it competitively, but if it's in a poor location, it may be your house longer than you want.

HomePrint Worksheet I: Defining Location

Selecting a location that will benefit your household now and your pocketbook when it comes time to sell are equally important. Rank the importance of the factors to your lifestyle (1 being least important) in order to help determine which locations best match these needs.

Ranking

Schools   1   2   3   4   5

If children are a part of your household, will the number in school increase or decrease in the next five years?   ☐ Yes   ☐ No
What special programs do you need?

_____

_____

_____

Do you have curriculum concerns or special needs? _____

_____

_____

_____

Are athletics important to you? What types of programs interest you? _____

_____

_____

_____

Proximity to Family   1   2   3   4   5

How often does your daily routine involve extended family members? Will you want to stay close to the family nucleus? How might these interactions change in a few years? Will you have aging parents to consider?

_____

_____

_____

Interests and Activities   **1 2 3 4 5**

Consider for each household member.

Where are your favorite cultural and social activities located?

_____

_____

Is location a factor in being able to enjoy hobbies and recreational activities? Do you want to be near parks, water, golf?

_____

_____

What organizations, clubs, or religious groups do you belong to? Where do they meet? What would you like to add?

_____

_____

Transportation   **1 2 3 4 5**

Consider for each household member.

Do you use public transportation?   ☐ Yes   ☐ No

Do you want to be close to an airport? ☐ Yes   ☐ No

How far are you comfortable driving for shopping and daily routine (dry cleaner, gas station, grocery stores)?

_____

_____

Working Style   **1 2 3 4 5**

Consider for each household member.

How far from work do you want to be? Do you work at home? Will your job likely change?

_____

_____

_____

Neighborhood   1   2   3   4   5

How long do you plan to live in this house? Is resale potential a
concern in the near future?

_____

_____

Consider the following demographics:
   Number of children in the neighborhood
   Median age of residents
   Median household income
   Educational background

Other Considerations   1   2   3   4   5

_____

_____

_____

List your top priorities across the top of the chart below, and neighborhoods or areas in the column on the left. Then check off which of those
priorities each location has to offer. Transfer the three locations that
meet the most of your needs to page 95.

Neighborhood	Our Lifestyle Priorities			
_____	_____	_____	_____	_____
_____	_____	_____	_____	_____
_____	_____	_____	_____	_____
_____	_____	_____	_____	_____
_____	_____	_____	_____	_____
_____	_____	_____	_____	_____

II. Determining What Type of House Will Make the Best Home

Now that you've narrowed down *where* you want to look, determining *what* you want to look for will seem easier. Evaluating your family and your lifestyle will likely have revealed the number of bedrooms, baths, and other characteristics that will make up your next house. Remember to consider your needs both now and in the next five years, plus the resale impact of specific decisions. For example, two bathrooms are "must haves" for most buyers; two-bedroom condos sell more quickly than one-; three-bedroom houses sell more quickly than two-. If you don't need the room now, what about the future? Is your family size likely to increase? Do you anticipate needing home office space? Will you have frequent overnight guests?

Now's the time to make your wish list. Don't forget the nine things you love, and don't be too conservative about what you wish for. A thorough list will help you prioritize and arrive at both a must have list and a secondary list of features you want but may be willing to forgo for others. This list will provide the basic parameters for selecting houses to tour.

The reason to prepare a detailed list now is that progressing from house*hunting* to house*buying* can, and usually does, happen in a heartbeat. Remember the two classic "Settling" situations. The *feeling* of home becomes so strong that you overlook the details or you get caught up in the feeling and the relief that you've found a house. The excitement and promise of a new space and new beginnings bring a powerful sense of optimism. Without an objective set of criteria—made when you're still in the planning stage—even seasoned buyers can get blindsided and overlook important elements.

I remember one such househunting experience when my children were small. I was a single parent at that time and looking to move closer to my family and into a better school district. I had a limited budget and simple objectives: I wanted a safe family neighborhood and a floor plan that would ease the chores involved in raising three young children. My agent had selected several properties that fit my budget and most of my criteria. The guidelines I had given him were centered on rooms rather than features: three bedrooms, two baths, first-floor family room, and a double garage. On the way to look at a house that had everything on the must have list, I noticed a house for sale that fit my picture of a family house: a brick Cape Cod with a bay window, a pretty yard, and in a neighborhood tucked away from busy streets. It

> Avoid move-in surprises with a thorough list of "must haves."

was as charming as anything I'd imagined, and I pleaded with the agent to stop on the spot and arrange for a showing. While he was calling his office, I scrutinized every detail of the outside: landscaping, color of the trim, the ivy growing on the garage, and the winding slate walk to the front door. The quiet street made the neighborhood feel safe. The houses were well kept, and I noticed a group of women walking by who appeared to be my age. As the agent told me the asking price was slightly out of my range, I was already wondering if I would qualify for a bigger mortgage.

When I walked into the house, I saw that it was more quaint than I had imagined: a fireplace, cove ceilings, and built-in china cabinets. When I stood in the breezeway, I pictured morning coffee and casual dinners with family and friends. I unconsciously reprioritized my list: the finished basement was substituted for the first-floor family room, the half-bath in the upstairs expansion area would suffice for several years until the children were older, and the single-car garage for a single-car family was hardly an issue. To my delight, my offer was accepted and the house was mine.

On moving day a few months later, I came across a box of dishes that had been misplaced. I asked my daughters to take it to the kitchen and put the dishes in the dishwasher. They returned with the dismal news: "Mom," they said, "we don't have a dishwasher!" How could I have missed such a key item—especially when one of my reasons for moving was to find a space that could ease the daily maintenance needs of a young family?

I had done what many buyers do: started out looking objectively and lost my heart and my list at the same time. I moved instantly through the househunting stage and concentrated my energy on finding a way to make the house work financially. Certainly a dishwasher does not a house make, and in the bigger picture the house itself had something much more important: it *felt* like home. We lived in the house for eight years, until we outgrew it. We added the dishwasher (and a double garage), but not for several years because I had stretched my income to make the purchase. It's very likely I would still have bought the house if I'd been aware that it lacked a dishwasher; however, having a detailed and prioritized list would have made the compromise conscious. My list had been focused on much broader criteria: a neighborhood and a floor plan that would make life less hectic. A closer look at secondary criteria would have prompted a more detailed list of what *features* could enhance my lifestyle.

Real estate experts know that a buyer forms an attitude—positive or negative—about a house within fifteen seconds of first seeing it and looks to reinforce that attitude through the rest of the tour. Buying strictly on emotion is like impulse buying in the checkout line. You wouldn't make other significant purchases—such as a car, furniture, or major appliances—in this manner. A house should be no different.

Making a thorough list now will also help you cut through the confusion when you find several houses you like. You can measure each property against your criteria to narrow the choice to one or two that have most of what you're looking for.

When a client divorced several years ago, he decided to move to a condominium. Increasing medical problems had made yard work and the general upkeep of a single-family home too difficult and time-consuming for him. His search focused on finding a unit of the size he wanted in a location near his golf club and his family. The one he found seemed perfect, yet he never appeared to be very happy with his space. An outgoing, social person, he didn't entertain friends and seldom even invited family members to his home.

After three or four years he admitted that the condo hadn't been a wise choice. He felt isolated and closed in. While he didn't want yard work, he had loved the social interaction with neighbors. A condo on the fifth floor didn't provide for such an option. He actually missed some of the maintenance because it kept him active. After much thought he decided that a town house would have been a better choice. He could have the freedom from heavy yard work but enjoy the beauty of flowers and the direct access to the outdoors. He could do more maintenance than change a lightbulb and feel a greater sense of ownership than in a condo. He moved after four years and has lived happily in his town home for over eight years. The container garden on his patio is a showcase, and he's built strong friendships with his neighbors.

Style and Condition

Worksheet 11 on pages 59 to 62 will help you define what types of houses to look at. What style do you prefer? Older with extensive wood and filled with nooks and crannies, or the cleaner lines and open spaces of contemporary?

When defining the type of home you want, consider the interaction of features and amenities. Realistically evaluate the impact of not having a yard to maintain. Is it worth giving up the resulting activities and interaction? What type of house will provide the best middle ground? If you love the feeling of an older home, are you willing to accept the likelihood of increased maintenance and repairs? Will you have the time and the budget to keep up with such demands? Or, if you're thinking of looking at houses in need of repair or cosmetic changes, be certain to provide for the financial commitment on Worksheet III.

Floor Plan, Lot, and Features

In addition to your general architectural preferences and the types of home-based activities you enjoy, what kind of floor plan will most benefit your household now and in the next five years? If you have or are planning to have children, will you want an open floor plan that allows you to keep an eye on younger family members? If your household includes teens, do you want a home with private spaces to provide quiet for studies or freedom for individual (theirs *and* yours!) music enjoyment? Will you be faced with caring for older parents in the near future, or do you have live-in help or an au pair? Perhaps a home with a separate wing, or even a "mother-in-law apartment," will make this transition easier for everyone.

The floor plan of a house can strengthen the interaction of a household.

The objective of this section of your HomePrint is to prioritize features and provide a structure for your search, yet allow you to remain flexible enough for compromise when you see a home you love, and ultimately to assist you in clearly evaluating your options. Make notes on how you use each room and feature now. How might it change in the next five years? How do you entertain? Do you need a space for hobbies? What would you do with extra space? Make notes under each room and area of specific features and amenities that would enhance their appeal. Do you long for a dining room with built-in china cabinets? What features do you want in a kitchen? What type of entertaining do you do most often—formal or informal, large groups or small intimate gatherings? What type of space supports your hobbies now, or what might you take up if you had different space? How do you use a yard now, or how might you in the future?

When you've completed your list of must-haves and wish-it-would-haves on your HomePrint worksheet, evaluate it against your Game of Nines. Is the type of house you've defined supportive of the activities you love? Ask yourself, If I found the house, how would my list of nines change? When you're done rank the importance of each item and choose the top five features you want in your next house.

Remember, no house will be perfect. Your HomePrint will serve as a yardstick against which to evaluate the properties you consider, not as a concrete list of must haves.

HomePrint Worksheet II: What Type of House Will Make the Best Home?

It's important to choose a house that will help support and enhance the lifestyle you envision for yourself and your family—today, and in years to come. To help winnow out those features that matter most to you and avoid later disappointments, consider the following, rating each feature in terms of its overall importance to you. Note the five most important in the spaces indicated at the end: this is your "must have" list.

	1	2	3
	Don't Care	Nice to Have	Must Have

Style and Condition

Type: 1   2   3

☐ Condo   ☐ Town house   ☐ Single family

Architectural preferences: 1   2   3

☐ Traditional   ☐ Contemporary

   ☐ Other: _____   1   2   3

Age: 1   2   3

☐ Older   ☐ Newer

Condition: 1   2   3

☐ Move in   ☐ Fix up

   ☐ Will you look at houses in need of cosmetic changes?

   ☐ Repair?

The Basics

Bedrooms: Number _____

	1	2	3
☐ Guest/spare room _____	1	2	3
☐ Master suite _____	1	2	3
☐ Children's wing _____	1	2	3
☐ Walk-in closets _____	1	2	3
☐ Live-in help or mother-in-law apartment _	1	2	3
☐ Other wishes: _____	1	2	3

Bathrooms: Number _____

	1	2	3
☐ Powder room _____	1	2	3
☐ Separate shower/tub _____	1	2	3
☐ Double sinks _____	1	2	3

☐ Linen closet _____	1	2	3
☐ Spa/whirlpool _____	1	2	3
☐ Other wishes: _____	1	2	3

Kitchen:

☐ Eating space _____	1	2	3
☐ Special appliances _____	1	2	3
☐ Island _____	1	2	3
☐ Pantry _____	1	2	3
☐ Storage _____	1	2	3
☐ Lighting _____	1	2	3
☐ Other wishes: _____	1	2	3

Entertaining/Leisure Spaces

☐ Formal dining room _____	1	2	3
☐ Family room/great room _____	1	2	3
☐ Other: _____	1	2	3

Additional Spaces

☐ Den/media room/study _____	1	2	3
☐ Home office _____	1	2	3
☐ Exercise room _____	1	2	3
☐ Hobby room _____	1	2	3
☐ Laundry space _____	1	2	3
☐ Mud room _____	1	2	3
☐ Play space _____	1	2	3
☐ Storage space _____	1	2	3
☐ Basement/attic _____	1	2	3
☐ Garage/parking _____	1	2	3
☐ Other: _____	1	2	3

Outdoor Spaces

☐ Yard size: _____ Fenced? _____   1   2   3

☐ Garden/landscaping _____   1   2   3

☐ Play space _____   1   2   3

☐ Entertaining/leisure _____   1   2   3

☐ Patio _____   1   2   3

☐ Deck _____   1   2   3

☐ Porch _____   1   2   3

☐ Pool _____   1   2   3

☐ View _____   1   2   3

☐ Other: _____   1   2   3

Other Features and Wishes

☐ Fireplace _____   1   2   3

☐ Hardwood floors _____   1   2   3

☐ Built-in china cabinets/buffet _____   1   2   3

☐ Central air _____   1   2   3

☐ Other: _____   1   2   3

Association Services

Security _____   1   2   3

Transportation _____   1   2   3

Concierge _____   1   2   3

Health club _____   1   2   3

The Top Five Features for Our Lifestyle

1. ....

2. ....

3. ....

4. ....

5. ....

III. Estimating Your Buying Power

Finally, how *much* house you can purchase will further identify which houses to tour. The financial element relates directly to both where you want to live and the type of house you can purchase in that location. Consider more than your current debt when arriving at a desired monthly mortgage payment. Your financial situation frequently determines your quality of life.

"House poor" has taken on a different meaning than it had when I bought my first house at age twenty-one. Then it was common, even considered wise, to stretch your budget if your prospects for increased income appeared bright. The first year or two required some sacrifices, but the road was easy when the percentage of income needed for a mortgage payment decreased. Times have changed. First-time homebuyers are older (in 1996 the average age of a first-time buyer in the United States was thirty-two, compared with age twenty-eight in 1976). In just ten years the average price of first-time houses has risen nearly 70 percent, to $152,900. The healthy economy and new options for borrowing down payments or using 401(k) funds have provided buyers with more cash, allowing them to purchase more expensive homes.

Thirty years ago a starter home was modest; today it can be of mansion proportions. If you've driven by some new housing developments lately, you may have wondered how such young families afford such grand homes. A look inside might reveal that life isn't as it seems. The new house poor have stretched their budgets so far that even basic furniture and decorating isn't an option. Underestimating the costs of routine maintenance, unexpected repairs, or furnishing a large space has resulted in lifestyles less than they imagined.

> A mortgage should support—not dictate—your lifestyle.

When you calculate your buying power, consider more than how much mortgage you can qualify for. How will this new payment affect your lifestyle? Are you willing to make the sacrifices? Remember, this probably won't be your last house. Do you have enough furniture for the house you want, or will you need to budget for major purchases, too? Will you have to sacrifice hobbies, recreation, or entertainment? How important are they? How much will you want to spend each year on vacations? Do you foresee other major purchases or commitments in the next few years? For example, will you be needing another car? Will you have a child going off to college? Are your savings, investment, and retirement plans adequate, or do you want to increase your contributions? Nothing causes stress like financial pressure and the frustration of feeling housebound because your budget is stretched too far. You may be able to *afford* a large mortgage payment, but is it worth it if the payment will confine your lifestyle rather than provide for a house that enhances it?

House poor is life poor.

The length of your mortgage can also affect your discretionary income and how quickly you build equity. Fifteen- and twenty-year mortgages are gaining in popularity because they reduce debt more quickly and correspondingly reduce total interest considerably. The trade-off is, of course, that monthly payments are much higher—20 percent or more—and your income must be higher to support the payments. A shorter-term mortgage is a good option if you have the budget flexibility; however, you can accomplish the same result with a little discipline. Either invest additional funds elsewhere each month or make additional principal payments when you're able. Most mortgages allow prepayment.

A client of mine recommends making biweekly mortgage payments to accomplish a similar objective: divide your mortgage payment in half and make a partial payment every two weeks, making certain that you pay the total monthly amount by the due date. The effect will be one additional payment each year, resulting in a faster reduction of principal and a significant savings on interest. You may be able to structure your mortgage for biweekly payments, or you can follow your own plan as your finances and circumstances allow.

The HomePrint Worksheet III on page 69 will help you roughly calculate the mortgage you can carry and the price range you can afford. Start by calculating your total monthly gross income. Then figure the percentage of your income allowable as a monthly mortgage payment using two methods: 36 percent of gross, less current monthly liabilities, or a flat 28 percent of gross, which translates into a mortgage payment equal to approximately one week's earnings. Lenders will use the lower of the two methods to arrive at a maximum allowable monthly mortgage payment, including principal, interest, taxes, and insurance.

How Much Down Payment Shall I Make and Where Can I Get It?

Your down payment will usually determine the types of mortgages you will qualify for. (See "Choosing the *Right* Mortgage," page 86, for an overview of mortgages and the general requirements of each.) How much cash you have or can borrow will determine your maximum down payment. Determining how much money you will actually use as a down payment involves looking at several factors, including the impact of the down payment on the interest rate and terms of a mortgage and the impact of the monthly payment on your lifestyle.

Down payment requirements can vary from nothing down for a VA loan and some first-time–buyer assistance to 20 percent for a conventional mortgage. A new mortgage, "Flexible 97," broadens home-ownership opportunities with down payment requirements as low as 3 percent and more flexible rules regarding the source of the funds. If your down payment is less than 20 percent, you will have to carry private mortgage insurance (PMI) until the equity in your home reaches 20 percent. Private mortgage insurance protects the lender against loan default and is required on most mortgages, except VA loans, because historically more defaults occur when homeowners have less than 20 percent equity in their home. This insurance is good for the lender, but you pay for it, and it's expensive. It may allow you to get into more house with less down, but it also results in a higher mortgage payment. So if putting down a few thousand dollars more makes the difference between having to carry this insurance or not, it's usually worth increasing your down payment.

In addition to your own cash, you can also use a cash gift from a relative or withdraw funds from a 401(k) plan to use as down payment. If you use a cash gift, obtain a certified cashier's check payable to you and a gift letter (your lender will give you the language to use) to show that the funds are a gift, not a loan that would increase your debt. You'll need to bring the cashier's check and gift letter to your closing. Don't just deposit the check in your bank account, because then you will need to obtain a copy of the canceled check and your bank statement or deposit receipt showing the deposit into your account in addition to a gift letter. If you plan to withdraw funds from your 401(k), start the process now. It can take up to a month to receive the money.

If you've owned a house before, you'll be more likely to have ample cash for a down payment and will have more flexibility on the amount you decide to use. Purchasing your house with a smaller down payment will free cash to decorate or renovate now rather than later; or perhaps you want to invest some of the profit from your last house. On the other hand, a larger down payment can mean a lower interest rate and lower monthly payments, leaving more money for short-term expenditures such as vacations.

Calculate the effects of different down payments on your monthly budget and long-term financial goals. Generally speaking, the money you put down on a house won't appreciate as quickly as investing it. On average houses appreciate 3 percent a year and will do so regardless of how much down payment you make. But if your goal is to pay the house off as quickly as possible, a larger down payment and short-term mortgage is the way to

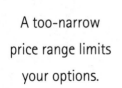

Put your down payment to the best possible use.

go. When you meet with a lender, you can determine what down payment amount will obtain the best mortgage to enhance your lifestyle.

Price Range

Establishing a price range about 10 percent below and above your maximum mortgage calculation will increase your options when you're househunting. Because many sellers expect to negotiate, the asking price of a house may be somewhat higher than the expected selling price—so the list price may be out of your range, but the final selling price may not. Also, don't hesitate to look at houses on the low end of your price range— you may uncover a bargain. For example, a house in great condition might be priced at the high end of *its* price range but the low end of *yours*. If that house is in a neighborhood of larger, more expensive houses, you may have more flexibility to make changes

A too-narrow price range limits your options.

that will return your investment. Likewise, a house at the high end of your price range but the low end of the neighborhood range, and in need of some work may be your ticket to increasing equity more quickly if you enjoy updating and decorating. A few thousand dollars on the listing or sale price may translate into only a few dollars on a monthly payment, and creative financing may put you into more house than you'd imagined possible.

When you have completed this worksheet, it's time to do a reality check. Compare the summary information on each of your three worksheets. Review each element in relation to the others, then prioritize all three. Will one good location allow you to buy more house than another? How important is the *kind* of house versus the location? Does your buying power support the picture of the house you want, where you want it, and the lifestyle you want to have in it? When you are comfortable with the balance of the three components, transfer the information to the HomePrint Summary on page 95.

You're now started in the right direction. In the next chapter you'll see how the assistance of professionals can expedite your househunting process and reduce the stress of waiting to find out if the house that matches your HomePrint will become yours. Step Two, "Assembling Your Resources," will strengthen your position as a homebuyer. Now you'll look at houses with a sense of comfort and confidence that this house will be your best purchase yet!

HomePrint Worksheet III: Estimating Your Buying Power

Determining a realistic price range will further focus your search. When you've estimated your buying power, measure it against your location and features lists. How realistic are your priorities?

	Buyer 1	Buyer 2
Income		
Annual gross salary	_____	_____
(include all income sources for each borrower, but do not include onetime gifts, capital gains, inheritance, or insurance settlements)		
Other annual income:		
Dividends, interest	_____	_____
Social security benefits	_____	_____
Rental income	_____	_____
Child support	_____	_____
Other	_____	_____
Total	_____	_____
Joint total	$_____	
Divide by 12	÷ 12	
Gross Monthly Income	$_____	

Now calculate your desired monthly payment

	36% Method	28% Method
Gross monthly income	_____	_____
Multiply by	× .36	× .28

Monthly housing and long-term

debt allowance = _____

Subtract current monthly debt:

Auto − _____

Credit cards − _____

Loans − _____

Child support − _____

Monthly portion of quarterly

or annual payments − _____

Other − _____

Total − _____

Monthly housing budget
(including principal, interest,
taxes, and insurance) = _____   _____

Continue with the lesser of the two figures $_____

Subtract allowance for other expenses
(savings, vacations, tuition, decorating and furnishings, etc.)

_____ − _____

_____ − _____

_____ − _____

Your Desired Monthly Housing Expenditure $ _____

                                                      × .80

*(About 20 percent will be needed for taxes and insurance,
leaving 80 percent for mortgage principal and interest.)*   _____

Divide by the interest rate factor from
the chart on page 72   _____

Multiply by $1,000   × 1,000

Maximum mortgage amount   _____

Add your down payment   + _____
(see page 65)

Estimated Purchase Price $ _____
*(Remember, this is a general calculation because the taxes and
interest rates won't be exact until you find a specific house.)*

Our Estimated Buying Power

Desired monthly mortgage payment $ _____

Estimated maximum mortgage $ _____

+ Down payment $ _____

= Estimated purchase price $ _____

Price range (± 10% of purchase price):

$ _____   to $ _____

Interest Rate Factor Chart

Use this chart to calculate your monthly principal and interest payments for fifteen- and thirty-year loans. Find today's interest rate, then choose the corresponding fifteen-year or thirty-year factor according to the length of mortgage you want. Enter this factor on Worksheet III (on page 71).

Interest Rate	15-Year Mortgage	30-Year Mortgage	Interest Rate	15-Year Mortgage	30-Year Mortgage
4.00	7.40	4.77	8.00	9.56	7.34
4.25	7.52	4.92	8.25	9.70	7.51
4.50	7.65	5.07	8.50	9.85	7.69
4.75	7.78	5.22	8.75	9.99	7.87
5.00	7.91	5.37	9.00	10.14	8.05
5.25	8.04	5.52	9.25	10.29	8.23
5.50	8.17	5.68	9.50	10.44	8.41
5.75	8.30	5.84	9.75	10.59	8.59
6.00	8.44	6.00	10.00	10.75	8.77
6.25	8.57	6.16	10.25	10.90	8.96
6.50	8.71	6.32	10.50	11.05	9.15
6.75	8.85	6.48	10.75	11.21	9.33
7.00	8.99	6.65	11.00	11.36	9.52
7.25	9.13	6.82	11.25	11.52	9.71
7.50	9.27	6.99	11.50	11.68	9.90
7.75	9.41	7.16	11.75	11.84	10.09

CHAPTER 4

Step Two:
Assembling Your Resources

There's much more to buying a house than hopping in a car on a Sunday afternoon and going to a few open houses. Your HomePrint is designed to make the actual househunting more focused and fun for the entire household. Savvy homebuyers go one step further and put their ducks in a row before they hit the streets: they make the most of the resources available in the real estate industry. From agents to mortgage lenders and home inspectors to tax accountants, and financial advisers, the services and assistance of professionals increase your probability of smooth sailing through the homebuying process. Having your financing in order and your current house well positioned and priced right before buying will minimize frustration and maximize your options when you find the house you want to buy. This step will strengthen your position as a buyer and ensure that you are able to act quickly and confidently when you find a house that meets your criteria.

A woman attending one of my seminars recently told me the story of her last move. After contemplating a move for several years, she and her husband had decided to downsize. They planned to sell their longtime family home in the suburbs and purchase a duplex or town house in the city. Their timing was somewhat flexible, so they had the luxury of preparing a schedule that would be least disruptive to their busy lives. They allowed three months to get ready to sell and planned to start looking for a house in earnest as soon as theirs was ready for market. They also wanted to purchase all new furnishings and decided to sell their home on their own to maximize their profits.

Two months before their house was ready for market, they grew more anxious to start looking for a new home. They looked at dozens of duplexes, town houses, and condominiums, but nothing seemed to fit. In one duplex the bedrooms were too small, in another they didn't have private access to the backyard, and the older condominiums shared a laundry room. One afternoon on the way to a movie, they stopped at a for-sale-by-owner open house "just to look." It stole their hearts the moment they walked in. Although it wasn't a duplex or town house, it had every feature they wanted: it was smaller and more manageable; it had a renovated kitchen, a quaint atmosphere that felt comfortable, and an elegance that fit the style of furnishings they envisioned purchasing. As they walked through the rooms, they reveled in the quiet of no one above or next to them and knew they weren't ready to "share" a house. As a bonus the price had just been reduced that day, and they were convinced they'd save two real estate commissions by purchasing directly from the owner. They made an offer contingent on the sale of their house and accelerated their selling plan.

Two days before the scheduled open house, the sellers of their new house received another offer, and the couple had seventy-two hours to remove the contingency. Luckily, their suburban house sold in a matter of days with just one hitch: the buyers wanted possession in three weeks! They discussed the timing with the sellers of their new house. Fortunately they, too, wanted to move quickly and agreed to an earlier closing.

It had been more than ten years since this couple had bought or sold a house, and they were totally unprepared for the whirlwind weeks ahead. They didn't know the next step, and they didn't have an agent to help—on either end! They hadn't taken the time for a mortgage preapproval, which meant starting at the beginning of the process. Because they were self-employed, the mortgage application process was lengthy and complex. The volume of information requested was phenomenal, and their stress level rose each day. They even decided to forgo a home inspection just to reduce the number of details to coordinate. In the end their mortgage application couldn't be processed quickly enough to meet the closing date, but the sellers agreed to rent the house to them until a new closing date was arranged.

The story has a happy ending: they love their house although they paid a heavy emotional price. Both agreed that the course they chose had made the process more difficult—they broke all the rules of housebuying! They could have avoided the extraordinary stress had they been better prepared. First, they'd *assumed* they were ready to downsize. After looking at dozens of smaller houses and not finding anything, a reassessment would have refocused their search. Second, in addition to the anxiety of buying a house on a contingency, not obtaining mortgage preapproval resulted in more stringent time demands than they had anticipated.

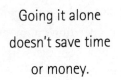

Going it alone doesn't save time or money.

Not assembling professional resources costs both time and money. Without the time savings of a preapproval, they incurred the additional expense of renting for over a month. Forgoing a home inspection meant forgoing the peace of mind that they'd made a sound purchase. Not to mention that an inspection would have uncovered a bat's roost that cost over a thousand dollars to remove! The assumption that purchasing from a for-sale-by-owner would save money and time was false. (It is unlikely that any homeowner is selling on his own for the fun of it and discounting the price of the house by the amount of a real estate commission.) An agent would have taken charge of the details. Any commission paid would have been less than the stress toll.

Now this woman and her husband were selling again and were determined to do their homework and work with professionals to avoid the stress they had previously endured.

Deciding *How* to Look for a House: On Your Own or with an Agent?

While I understand why some homeowners choose to try *selling* a house on their own, I fail to see the logic in *buying* a home without an agent—even if you buy one that is offered for sale by the owner. I'm a firm believer in purchasing the expertise of professionals: attorneys, tax accountants, business consultants, *and* real estate agents. Having experienced the consequences of proceeding on my own—from trying to sell a house alone to signing a contract without an attorney—I'm convinced that it is far more expensive in time, aggravation, and money to try to handle major purchases and issues without professional advice and assistance. What you don't know *can* hurt you, particularly in the real estate environment, where changes in the laws and options occur almost daily. If you're like me, you have your own changing environment to keep pace with!

Working with an Agent

It's a fact: most houses—about 80 percent—are sold through real estate professionals. With information from your HomePrint, an agent can search for listings that fit your guidelines and pretour houses to provide you with a firsthand assessment—*before* you spend valuable time looking at houses that don't match your criteria. An agent can also provide access to more houses, faster. Agents are constantly monitoring the Multiple Listing Service (MLS) to find new houses for their customers. Without access to that information on a timely basis, you won't see a house until, and unless, it is advertised in the newspaper or you drive by an open house. Many desirable houses sell long before the sign goes up or an ad is placed in the newspaper. Without an agent you'll never even know they were for sale.

> Time and timeliness are an agent's gift to homebuyers.

In working with the real estate industry since the 1980s, I've seen a new breed of agents. They're professional, knowledgeable, and don't fit the old stereotypes. Part-time agents are becoming a thing of the past, and more and more new agents are choosing careers in real estate right out of college.

Of course, when engaging any service professional you'll want to thoroughly check references. Good agents will have strong reputations and references that document their value. Finding the right house depends on good communication, so you'll want to be comfortable that your needs and wants are understood. Good agents will probably listen more than talk, and they'll respond by showing you homes that demonstrate they understood. Agents tend to specialize in certain geographic areas, so you'll want to be confident that the agent you select is well established where you're looking. Being open and honest about what you like and don't like will help your agent do the best possible job. If you don't feel your needs are being addressed or if you feel under any pressure, talk with your agent about your concerns. Or find another—there are many agents available who will fit your style of doing business.

Buyer's Versus Seller's Agents

Sometime during the course of looking for an agent or attending an open house, you'll hear the term *buyer's agent, seller's agent,* or *dual agency.* Generally, if you hire a buyer's agent you'll sign an agreement to work exclusively with him or her for a certain period of time. The agreement will prohibit the buyer's agent from disclosing confidential information to the seller. Compensation for this service is negotiable, varying from sharing in the selling commission (meaning you won't pay anything) to a fee or retainer.

Dual agency is when the broker represents both the buyer and the seller. It can occur, for example, when an agent who lists the property also finds a buyer for it. Or it can occur when both the agent representing the seller and the agent representing the buyer work for the same firm. If an agent has agreed by contract to represent the seller, he or she cannot also represent the buyer unless both buyer and seller agree. If you have any questions about who an agent or broker is representing, ask.

Teamwork Goes Both Ways

You may be tempted to work with several agents, believing that the more people who are looking for you, the faster you'll find a house. In fact, the opposite may be true. When one of the agents calls to tell you about a new listing and you already have an appointment to see it with another, you can bet that agent won't continue investing the time to keep your interests first! Loyalty is a key element in a service relationship. When you find an agent you trust, let him or her work for you. Call if you see a house you like, whether it's a for sale by owner or another company's listing, and let your agent research the details before you go

> Loyalty is the price of good service.

off on a tangent. Where a loyal relationship exists, you'll find most agents more than willing to go the extra mile for you.

As a buyer the service you can expect from an agent is extensive. An agent will assess your financial situation and make financing suggestions. He can provide extensive information on neighborhoods and take you touring to compare locations. For example, he can provide the statistical information on neighborhood demographics, schools, selling trends, and crime rates. In addition to monitoring new listings and pretouring houses, your agent's "resale perspective" can help you evaluate the house you want. You'll have the benefit of his objective expertise to help you negotiate the contract, and he can give you access to a wealth of resources within the industry.

From home inspectors to attorneys, title insurance companies, and mortgage lenders, your agent and her network will save you time and frustration—and probably some money. And the relationship doesn't have to end when you get the keys to your new house. Closing on a house doesn't mean closing relationships. Good agents can provide assistance between the time you buy and the time you're ready to sell again, from networks of other professionals you may need as a homeowner to ongoing information about the market and when is the best time to sell. You'll have worked closely with your agent during an intense time. She'll learn your needs—and your idiosyncrasies. I have many clients who tell me that their closest friends were once customers.

When you've completed your HomePrint Summary, review it with your agent to send him or her off in the right direction to find your new home.

Looking on Your Own

If you decide not to work with an agent, where do you start? First, gather your resources *before* looking for a house: select a lender and get preapproved for a loan (see the next section), choose

Choosing a Real Estate Agent

Use these guidelines to select and evaluate a real estate professional:

- Talk with friends, neighbors, and co-workers who have recently bought or sold homes. With whom did they work? What was their experience?

- Take note of company names on SOLD signs in your area. Call the most active companies and ask for a recommendation of an agent who is best suited to your specific needs.

- If you're new to the city, ask for a referral from an agent in your town whom you know and trust. Most real estate companies share extensive national referral networks.

- Interview at least three agents and evaluate them by their responses to your questions and by the questions they ask *you*.

Here are some important questions for you to ask:

- ✓ What are your qualifications, experience, and education?
- ✓ How long have you been a real estate agent?
- ✓ Do you specialize in specific areas? How do you keep abreast of the workings of a community and aware of issues that might affect property values?

Here are some topics agents should discuss with you:

- ✓ Your state's law of agency. Did the agents disclose for whom they are working? How clearly was the information presented?
- ✓ Your financial information. This is critical for an agent to provide the best service.
- ✓ Your needs in a home. A thorough understanding of your household's needs is essential to effectively research

houses to show. The best agents will preview properties
before taking you on tour.

✓ Above all, how comfortable are you having this person
represent you? Are you confident the service you'll receive
will be an asset to your homebuying venture?

a home inspector, check with your tax adviser, and hire a real estate
attorney. With these professionals in place, you'll be ready to
respond when you find a house you like.

The best places to start looking are the Sunday newspaper real
estate section and open houses. Driving through neighborhoods in
the areas you've selected can also reveal houses that are for sale but
not advertised.

The Internet is a fun way to get a quick overview of the market.
You'll still need to contact an agent for a showing or the seller if the
house is a for sale by owner, but you can search by your price range
and get an idea of what's available. Most national and regional companies and many individual agents have Web sites. The National
Association of Realtors' site, realtor.com, has extensive information
on listings—over one million property ads are featured, and the
number is growing. Nearly every state in the United States, plus
Canada and Puerto Rico, participates. From this site, and many individual company sites, you can also access decision-support services
for homebuyers, including a mortgage calculator and comparisons
of the cost of living in various locations.

Keep in mind that unless the house is a for sale by owner, the
agents you call will be seller's agents. When you find a house to purchase, have your real estate attorney draw up the purchase agreement for you and work with your other resources to help guide you
through the process. The money you spend on these services will be
wisely invested.

Getting Your Financing in Order

To avoid looking at houses you can't afford—or possibly looking at less house than you *can* afford—confirm that the price range you've calculated is accurate. The easiest way to make sure your financial picture is in focus is to be preapproved for a loan. A mortgage preapproval will make certain that you are looking in an affordable price range and that you won't be waiting anxiously for a loan approval after you find a house.

You must apply for a mortgage sooner or later. Pre*approval* means you can go househunting with a commitment for a specific mortgage amount. You'll complete an application, and the lender will process it, obtaining a credit report and verifying your employment, assets, and debts. Preapproval generally takes about a week, although I've known some cases when it's been a matter of hours. That week can cut a month or more out of the time line between when your offer is accepted and when you close on your house—not to mention adding to your peace of mind. When you've been preapproved the only mortgage detail left is for the lender to order the appraisal and title work. It's that simple. And it could get easier and take less time in the future if the house you choose has been preappraised and preinspected—a move by industry leaders to streamline the real estate transaction process.

Increase your popularity with preapproval.

Applying sooner and being preapproved also makes you a very desirable buyer. It can mean a seller accepting your offer over that of another buyer who has yet to demonstrate the capability of purchasing the home. In a hot market or with a hot property, preapproval can give you a definite edge.

When you are preapproved your loan officer will issue a letter stating you are preapproved for a certain amount. However, if you're approved for a mortgage of $200,000 and find a house at $175,000, don't hinder negotiations by disclosing the higher amount. When you find a house ask for a letter that confirms you're approved to purchase the property at the specific address for an amount equal to the figure your offer states you will finance. If you don't buy the house, your lender can change the amount and the property address and fax a new letter in a matter of minutes.

Pre*qualification* provides less definitive assurance. A loan officer will usually talk with you over the phone and will want to know how much you earn and what debts you have. He or she will request a credit report, and if it's acceptable you'll be prequalified. The lender will provide a letter, albeit vague, stating that subject to certain conditions you would qualify for an estimated mortgage amount. It won't guarantee that you'll get the mortgage, but it may demonstrate to a seller that you are a serious buyer. You can then begin shopping for a house and going through the preapproval process at the same time, completing the details while you're looking.

Prequalification isn't as strong as preapproval, but if your timetable is tight, it's certainly better than going into the market with nothing concrete to demonstrate to a seller that you are a ready, willing, and able buyer. Remember the for sale by owner who accepted an offer before my daughter's? He relied on a *prequalification* letter instead of *preapproval* documentation. When the buyer actually applied for a loan, he was not approved. Weeks later the seller contacted my daughter, but she had already made another decision. You can bet that seller wished that he hadn't relied on a prequalifying letter (or that he'd had an agent, who would have known the difference).

Selecting a Lender

Selecting a lender doesn't necessarily mean going to the bank anymore. Banks are still very active in the home mortgage arena, but there are also other players. *Mortgage bankers* make and service loans with their funds, or they may sell the mortgage and relend the money. If a mortgage banker turns you down, don't get discouraged; try a mortgage broker. *Mortgage brokers* work with several investors (banks and mortgage bankers) and match the special needs of borrowers with lenders.

When choosing a lender you'll want to compare interest rates, but you'll also want to consider service, reputation, and your comfort level. Interview three or four, and compare closing costs in addition to interest rates. Some lenders may advertise low rates and compensate with add-on fees. Look at all fees and ask which can be waived. If you find yourself having to pay three of the fees, consider another lender. These are the discretionary charges retained by a lender:

- Commitment fee ($175–$250). You may be charged this amount to lock in and secure an interest rate.
- Processing fee (approximately $150–$250). Lenders charge this fee when they don't have a loan processor on staff and must send the loan elsewhere and pay a fee for the processing service.
- Underwriting fee ($250–$350). Lenders may have to pay a premium when they have a file reviewed.
- Document preparation fee ($50–$200). This is just what it sounds like—the cost of preparing all the documents to complete the transaction.

A creative lender is a definite asset. He or she can help match a mortgage to your specific needs, obtaining the best interest rate and terms. For instance, a lender recently described how to avoid private mortgage insurance with a "piggyback" loan if you have less than the 20 percent down payment requirement. The lender makes an 80 percent loan, you come up with 10 percent, and the remaining 10 percent is acquired through a second mortgage on your new house. You can select a mortgage company for the second mortgage, or your lender can arrange it for you. There should be no closing costs on the second mortgage, and while your monthly payments may be higher to borrow the additional 10 percent, the interest on both loans will be tax deductible. What you pay for mortgage insurance is not. So in the end you'll save money. Piggyback loans are available in combinations other than 80-10-10.

A creative lender can unlock doors.

Shop around and you'll find that the industry is highly competitive and service oriented. Some lenders will take your application over the phone; ours actually came to our office to accommodate our busy schedules.

Also, check with your tax adviser now on the best way for you to take title of a house and any other considerations that could affect your total financial picture. A tax adviser's insight on the drawbacks and benefits of mortgages, size of down payment, and the implications of capital gains or losses for your particular circumstances will help you make wise decisions at crunch time.

Mortgage Application

Applying for a mortgage is much like applying for any type of loan, only it requires more documentation. Applying empty-handed will only mean that you'll have to assemble the documents and postpone the verification process. Gathering the documents

Choosing the *Right* Mortgage

When reviewing mortgage options consider how long you plan to live in the house, the down payment it will require, and how the monthly payment will affect your lifestyle. Will your financial situation be changing in a few years? How much risk are you willing to take? Compare each option and choose a mortgage that matches your lifestyle but doesn't determine it. Here are the basic categories:

Fixed Rate Loans. Consider a fixed rate loan if you wish to stabilize your housing expense or if you feel mortgage rates are low. Your interest and principal payment will remain the same throughout the term of the loan, usually fifteen or thirty years, although the rates will initially be higher than those of adjustable rate mortgages.

Adjustable Rate Mortgages (ARM). These mortgages are a good option if you don't plan to live in the house for a long period or if you expect interest rates to drop. An ARM starts with a low interest rate, which, after a specified period (one or more years), increases or declines based on the financial index used by your lender. Adjustable rate mortgages have caps on their interest rate increases, but their interest can—and usually does—rise to a point above what you could have obtained with a fixed rate mortgage. Be sure to consider the implications for you of unpredictable loan payments.

Lower initial monthly payments make qualifying for an ARM easier, so you may be able to afford a more expensive house. Analysts have determined that over the last twenty years homeowners have saved money with ARMs, particularly on large mortgages, where even a percentage of an interest point is significant. An ARM is not the most conservative approach to borrowing, but it can save you money.

Convertible ARMs. With these ARMs, the balance of your mortgage may be converted, after a waiting period, for the remaining term at the then applicable fixed rates. A premium and/or conversion fee may apply, but if you expect mortgage rates to decline you may save money by converting to a lower fixed rate mortgage later on.

FHA Loans. If you are short on cash or your credit rating is not well established, look at FHA loans. Smaller down payments are required, and they tend to be more lenient on credit, but you must buy mortgage insurance. The Federal Housing Administration (FHA) insures the lender against loss on these loans (both ARM and fixed rate).

VA (Veterans Administration) Loans. If you are a qualified veteran, go for it. With a VA loan it's possible to get into a house for absolutely nothing—not even closing costs—and there is no mortgage insurance. The VA mandates what types of charges can be added to a mortgage and partially guarantees these fixed-rate-only loans.

from the checklist on pages 88–89 before your initial interview will expedite the process and enable the lender to let you know immediately what additional information may be needed. And while organized and complete records don't make for a mortgage, they can relieve much of the stress of having to search for information knowing your application is sitting in someone's "pending" file.

Advance to "Go" with organized paperwork.

At the time of application you'll need to pay an application fee and/or the cost of a credit report. You typically won't have to pay for the appraisal until your offer is accepted. The lender will provide a good faith estimate of closing costs, which generally depend on the loan amount. It will detail the funds you will need at closing. The estimate will be updated when your actual down payment and mortgage amount are determined. Make sure you read everything you sign, and retain a copy of every document.

The interest rate at the time of your application may be different from the actual rate on your mortgage because rates fluctuate daily. When your offer is accepted you can "lock in," or secure a rate that will be good for a specified period, usually sixty days. Lenders tell me that when interest rates are on the rise, some buyers will lock in without having a property and pay a percentage of a point to secure a better rate. This isn't a common practice, but it's worth consideration if interest rates are rising quickly and you expect to find a house within thirty days.

Processing the application involves obtaining written verification of your employment, assets, and debts. Speed up the process by talking to the individual in your company who will receive the employment verification request and ask for a quick response.

Dot Your *i*'s and Cross Your *t*'s

Regardless of where you go for a loan, and what type of loan you choose, having your documentation organized and complete can speed up the process. Gather the following information prior to application:

At the preapproval stage:

✓ Check to cover the application fee

✓ Social security numbers of all borrowers

✓ Verification of income sources:

- Copy of a month's paycheck stubs
- If self-employed, two years' signed income tax returns
- W-2s for the past two years

✓ Names and addresses of current and former employers for the past two years

✓ Addresses and dates of residence for the past two years
✓ Mortgage company or landlord for the past two years:
  ● Account number
  ● Monthly payment
✓ Any other names under which you obtained credit
✓ Assets (bank accounts, stocks, IRAs, etc.):
  ● Financial institution name and address
  ● Account number
  ● Account balance
✓ Liabilities (loans, credit cards, etc.):
  ● Financial institution name and address
  ● Account number
  ● Account balance
✓ Other papers: copy of divorce decrees, bankruptcy papers, and a letter from the donor if your down payment is a gift

In addition to these items that can be gathered early, your lender will need the following to finalize your mortgage:
✓ Copy of the signed purchase agreement
✓ Copy of the listing agreement and contract for the sale of your current home
✓ Your canceled earnest money check or a copy if it hasn't cleared the bank. Keep a copy; you'll need it at closing

Understanding Your Purchase Agreement

The actual sale of a house occurs through a purchase agreement that sets forth the terms and conditions as agreed upon between you and the seller. A purchase agreement is binding and contains something in every paragraph that has a bearing on the purchase. The benefits of reading it now will be felt during one of the most intense times of the homebuying process: making the offer. Knowing the terminology and the choices you'll be facing will help you make clearer decisions when the decisions are many. You can obtain a standard purchase agreement at an office supply store or ask your agent for a copy. You're more likely to read it thoroughly when you're not in the heat of the buy, and you'll have more time now to obtain clarification on anything you don't understand.

The Home Inspector: Seeing a House Through Trained Eyes

A professional home inspection can uncover defects or potential problems in a house that may go undetected by an untrained eye and every purchase agreement should, whenever possible, contain a contingency that the property must pass inspection. The home inspection report will give you peace of mind if the house is trouble free, but if it reveals that the house is more than you bargained for, having included a home inspection contingency will give you options: you can ask the seller to make repairs, reduce the price commensurately, or cancel the contract. Remember, no house will be perfect; you should expect some minor flaws. Rest assured that most are easily remedied, but if you're unsure you'll want to obtain an estimate. Interviewing and choosing an inspector now will allow you to schedule the inspection immediately when your purchase agreement is signed.

A home inspector sees beyond a buyer's enthusiasm.

A client who works with relocating executives recently assisted a couple moving from another state. They had been transferred numerous times. Buying and selling houses was a way of life for them, and they were very systematic about the process—they knew what they wanted in a new home and selected a suburban area with

Choosing a Home Inspector

A professional home inspection will give you added assurance that the house you choose actually is as good as it looks. Here are some suggestions to help you hire a qualified inspector:

- Contact the American Society of Home Inspectors and ask for names of inspectors in your area. Members must have certain qualifications and conduct inspections that conform to set standards.
- Ask your agent for recommendations.
- Interview two or three inspectors and ask for references from homeowners in your area.
- Make certain the report you will receive will contain specific comments and not just a standard printout.
- Negotiate to include a return inspection after repairs have been made.

an abundance of upper-bracket listings. The search was routine and efficient, but it took a dramatic turn after the couple toured a house that the woman confided was *exactly* like her dream house.

The agent and couple prepared to make an offer. Because the house was new, had been built by a prestigious builder with an impeccable reputation, and had recently been inspected by the city for building code compliance, the couple wanted to save the expense of a home inspection. But their agent was insistent that they not cut corners on such a sizable investment. They agreed to hire an independent home inspector and returned to their out-of-state home to prepare for the move.

The inspector and the agent went through the house together. What should have been a routine inspection turned up an astonishing discovery: the main structural support beam had never been installed, and the house was already starting to sag! The agent personally delivered the report to the builder, who refused to believe it and promptly hired an engineer to prove the inspector wrong. No such luck. The engineer confirmed the inspector's findings. The builder agreed to correct the problem and warrant that the physical appearance of the house would not be affected.

Protecting Your Investment

While you won't need to make final insurance decisions at this time, knowing your options and responsibilities will save you time when there is less of it to make these necessary choices. Your lender will require proof of homeowners' insurance when you close on your new house. Just as with a mortgage, work with an insurance agent to tailor a policy that fits your needs. While the lender will be primarily concerned with structure replacement coverage, be sure that you also have adequate coverage for your possessions and that the policy includes liability insurance. The most common homeowners' policies package hazard, theft, vandalism, and liability coverage. Moving will be a good time to make an inventory of everything you own to be certain you're adequately covered. If you have jewelry or artwork valued over $1,000, check to see what is and isn't covered and include a valuable items rider.

Cover your assets.

Also ask your lender about title insurance requirements. Title insurance protects the title of your property against defects or outstanding claims on the property that might come up after the closing. The mortgage company will require it to protect its investment. At closing you will have the option of purchasing your own policy. If you're like most people, a house is the largest investment you will make. Protecting your ownership makes good sense. Title insurance is a onetime cost of a few hundred dollars (the price depends on the amount of the loan). Most standard policies have a number of exclusions. You may want to ask your real estate attorney to review the policy and negotiate to eliminate as many exclusions as possible and to include coverage for an increase in the value of your property.

Selling and Buying ... Timing Is Everything

In an ideal world transitions go smoothly. Your old house will sell just as you find a new one and both will close just as you are packed and ready to move. Realistically, timing the sale of one house to coincide with buying another is a bit more complicated. While it's ideal to sell your current house first, it isn't always practical. And although most offers will contain a contingency clause for selling an existing house, waiting for yours to sell before another buyer forces you either to remove the contingency or to give up the house is, at best, nerve-racking. The waiting game can also make you more apt to accept a less desirable offer on your current house just to avoid losing the new one. Or you can gamble on your house selling quickly, remove the contingency, and potentially be faced with two mortgage payments.

However, you can take steps to increase your odds of a fast and profitable sale. Every house will sell, of course. It's just a matter of when and for how much. And while no one can predict precisely when a house will sell, you aren't entirely at the mercy of the market. You can position your house to appeal to the broadest number of buyers by making certain it is in top condition and priced com-

> Well-positioned and priced right is half sold.

petitively. My Dress Your House for Success program is designed to decrease the time a house is on the market and increase the return on your investment by positioning it as a better value than the competition. Just like you, buyers will snap up a well-priced house in top condition.

I recently met a couple in one of my Dress Your House for Success seminars who were living a mortgage nightmare. They had owned both a family home in the suburbs and a lake cabin, where they spent summers and vacations. In recent years they'd put most of their effort into the lake home and decided to sell the house in the suburbs and purchase a town home in a new development. They lived in a desirable location but had not updated their house in over a decade. They were eager to move on and put their house on the market in "as is" condition. As you would expect, the house did not sell quickly, and they were soon faced with either proceeding on the purchase of the new town house or losing it. They went ahead with the new house, still believing the old one would sell regardless of condition. When I met them they'd been through several months of multiple mortgage payments—the suburban house, the lake house, *and* the new town home. The financial stress took its toll, and they were debating whether to lower the price of their old house or invest in making it more current to avoid further losses. They chose to do a little of both to effect a quick sale.

Few buyers can afford the burden of multiple house payments. And losing a house you had your heart set on is an emotional setback in the buying process. So if your situation includes selling your current home, don't focus all your attention on buying and leave the timing to chance. If you have the time, sell it first or include preparing your house for sale in your homebuying timetable.

HomePrint Summary

Make a copy of your HomePrint and this summary to give to your real estate professional and to add to the HomeFinders' Kit (see page 98).

The Top Three Locations for Our Lifestyle

1. _____
2. _____
3. _____

The Top Five Features We Want in Our Next House

1. _____
2. _____
3. _____
4. _____
5. _____

Our price range

$_____ to $_____

CHAPTER 5

Step Three:
Looking Through Walls

Y ou're now ready to enter the second phase of the homebuying process and embark on the adventure of searching for
the right house, in the right neighborhood, and at the right price.
As do most people, I find this phase thrilling although at times a bit
frustrating and confusing. But you've taken the time to build a solid
foundation. Your HomePrint will serve as a safety net to evaluate
your choices when the options are many. Having assembled your
resources, secured your financing, and prepared your old house to
sell quickly will position you as a solid, serious buyer when you step
into the market. You'll be a more thorough househunter when you
aren't wondering if your mortgage will be approved, and when
you're not trying to navigate the process alone. Best of all, you'll be
in control of the process and feel confident that you're well prepared
to make this significant purchase.

In a recent radio interview I was asked, "How can homebuyers
tell if the condition of the house they want to buy is really as good
as it seems, or if it has just been glossed over to *look* great?" The
answer was easy: "Hire a home inspector." The more difficult question is, How can buyers learn to look creatively at space to effectively
evaluate whether it will work for their household? Your ability as a

buyer to see *through* a seller's life—her belongings, decorating, and housekeeping—is a key attribute to being able to realistically evaluate the potential of a specific house as a home for your family. The suggestions that follow for looking creatively at houses will help you discover the *emotional* facets of a house, and the Househunters' Notes on page 115 will help you avoid confusion, remain objective, and stay in control of the decision process.

Looking Creatively—
Seeing What *Can Be* Instead of What *Is*

Unless a seller has prepared her house to assist you in imagining possibilities, you may well find it difficult to picture yourself living in someone else's space. If it's cluttered, it may feel small. If you don't like the seller's decorating style or taste in artwork, you may feel uncomfortable. If the house needs even minor repairs, you may wonder what else is wrong. You'll translate owning that house into a drain on your time and money—two precious commodities for homebuyers!

It's easy to become distracted by someone else's decor—personal items, collections, artwork, or even religious or political statements. Rather than see the house you are put off by styles or items because they are inconsistent with your own tastes or values. Remember, if this house becomes *your* house, it's *your* things you'll come home to.

The routines of daily living make a house a home.

Home is more than the structure. It's daily living and interaction. When touring a house stop in each room and try to imagine what it would feel like to live here. Mentally move in your furniture. Try to imagine more than the functional dimension of each room. For example, a kitchen is more than a work space. What will it be like on those evenings when your

The HomeFinders' Kit

To make the best use of your time, create a HomeFinders' Kit to take with you each time you venture out to look at houses. Put it all in a backpack or tote. Your kit should contain the following:

- A school-type folder with two pockets. One pocket can store the broker's listing sheets while the other should hold:
  - ✓ Ten copies of your Househunters' Notes (page 115). As you tour each house, complete the Househunters' Notes and attach them to the listing sheet along with any other information—photos, mortgage options, utility records, community description—given to you at the house. Be sure to make notes and rank each house as you tour.
  - ✓ A photocopy of a map of the city or area (your agent will be able to supply this). Mark each location you visit on the map and note other area attributes: schools, shopping, public transportation access, and any other attraction of interest to your household.
  - ✓ A copy of your HomePrint Summary and worksheets.
- Pen and extra sheets of paper or a legal pad.
- If you're touring with children, add fruit bars or juice. Just as they seem to have to use the bathroom in a store, children have a knack for becoming hungry when they tour a kitchen.
- Polaroid instant camera and film. If you don't have one it's a good investment for under $35. If you especially like a feature, take a photo and attach it to the listing sheet. A mini-album of each home you are considering can help jog your memory when the houses seem to blend together.

  (A video camera is another way to share a house if everyone in your household isn't able to tour.)

household comes together before a meal? Will it become a gathering place and facilitate impromptu conversation or an obstacle to interaction? Will it foster a cook's hobby or make meal preparation a chore? Where will you read the morning paper, and how would it feel to sip a cup of coffee in this room? Where does the light fall? Imagine specific activities: sitting around the dining room table with a group of friends, playing a rousing game of Scrabble in a family room, hanging out in a child's room or the yard, reading in a den. Where would an entertainment center fit, and how would it feel to relax and watch a movie here? What will holidays be like in this home? Would you feel proud to entertain family and friends here? Look, too, at daily maintenance routines: Will doing the laundry be expedited or become a drudgery, relegated to the dark and dingy area of a basement? What will the house be like during the hustle of work and school day mornings?

Does *your* life fit in this house?

While researching open houses for a recent video production, my partner and I toured numerous homes. I recall one house that was neat and clean, but the decor and furnishings were at odds with my taste. When the agent guided us into the kitchen and great room he said, "The owners tell me that they love to have coffee in front of the bay window and watch the deer in the early morning." That comment and the picture it painted changed my feeling of the room and inspired us to look at the remainder of the house with more enthusiasm for its potential. You won't always have the benefit of such visual descriptions, but you can get the same result by using your imagination.

Some houses will be more difficult to look at creatively. On the same research tour we approached the front door of an older urban home. Although the exterior was well kept, it was unadorned, and felt more like a one-dimensional photo than a welcoming home. We entered hesitantly, and the uncomfortable feeling continued. The hardwood floors had recently been refinished, and rather than go to the trouble of replacing furniture, the sellers had left everything in storage. Instead of admiring the newly finished floors, we felt uneasy, as if we had walked into a lifeless house. From that first impression we spent the remainder of our tour looking for what was *wrong* about the house instead of what was right. We didn't have to look for long. In one bedroom we were greeted by a wastebasket filled with beer cans and cigarette butts! In another, dirty laundry was strewn around. It's no wonder that the home had been on the market for over six months—no family would have been filled with enthusiasm when imagining their lives in that house.

Looking at a space creatively can be equally difficult in a well-dressed house. Here, you'll need to get beyond an owner's individual tastes and habits; looking at a house in black-tie condition requires disengaging—objectively stepping back and following your list *and* your heart. Think of how *your* furnishings will work. Will the room convey the same feeling? What will you have to add, and is it in your budget? Does this have the potential to be *your* house, or are you enamored by someone else's style and accessories? You can stay in control of both situations by assessing how any potential house measures up in the following objective categories.

> Don't be swayed by surface glamour.

Curb Appeal

Your first glimpse of a house delivers one of the strongest impressions it will make. Its appeal—how it makes you feel the moment you step out of your car—sets the tone for your entire tour. Those initial feelings form a basis for the viewpoint from which you evaluate every room and feature. If your first reaction is negative, pause and ask yourself why. Do the location, the neighborhood, and style of the house fit your criteria? If so give it another chance. If you don't like something about the exterior of a house, evaluate whether it's a major undertaking to correct or something that's easily remedied.

For example, I recently was asked to dress a 1950s home. The exterior was dark brown with a large metal awning. The half-dead shrubs and sparse flowers made it even more unattractive. Our crew of three transformed it in half a day: the metal awning came down easily and required just minor touch-up with paint we matched at the hardware store for $20. Another $20 for a gallon of light yellow paint on the shutters and trim brightened the entire facade. We spent $100 at the local farmers' market for shrubs and flowers. The dying bushes were replaced with variegated

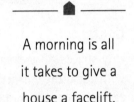

A morning is all it takes to give a house a facelift.

dogwood to counter the dark siding and complement the deep color of the healthy evergreens. A large clay pot planted with a small arborvitae and surrounded by pink petunias, asparagus ferns, and trailing white geraniums was placed at the front steps. A flat of pink and white petunias mixed with a flat of bright zinnias was planted along the front walk for instant, ongoing color. Old English Scratch Cover and twenty minutes gave the dull and faded front door a warm glow. In another twenty minutes we polished the house numbers, added a colorful welcome mat, and hung a basket of moss roses from the mailbox. Total cost: under $200.

Other economical ways to improve the exterior of a dull or dated house include a new door knocker, a seasonal wreath, and a fresh coat of paint on a door. New lighting fixtures or walkway lights add ambience to any exterior while providing added security. A few bags of new bark or cocoa shells give a contemporary look to landscaping. Groupings of clay pots can be used from year to year and planted with seasonal flowers. Window boxes are an inexpensive way to add dimension and style to a stark facade.

On the other hand, if it's love at first sight, rely on your planning efforts. Tour the house several times, comparing your Househunters' Notes (see page 115) against your HomePrint worksheets to be certain that a specific feature or general ambience hasn't overshadowed your priorities. Remember the story on page 54 of the house I fell in love with before I walked in the front door? Because the appeal from the curb was so strong, I toured the house looking through rose-colored glasses. I lost my heart and my list at the same time.

Clutter

Any space will feel smaller when it looks disorganized or is filled with furniture, plants, collections, and photos. Even extra doors, common in older homes, can make a space feel smaller. To counter the cramped feeling of clutter, refer back to the statistics of the house and the room dimensions. Compare the dimensions with those of your current house or a house you are familiar with and try to visualize how the space might be used if it weren't all taken. Do the overall dimensions of the rooms and house meet your criteria? Remember, you're buying a house, not everything in it. One of the terms of the sale will be that the sellers remove *all* their possessions; looking beyond them may uncover a great floor plan.

> Clutter can hide a world of charm and space.

A San Francisco television station recently asked me to put my Dress Your House for Success process to the test. The producer selected a house for sale for me to evaluate with "buyers' eyes" and make recommendations to improve its marketability. I knew exactly what to look for: exterior maintenance areas that spell w-o-r-k, clutter that makes rooms feel smaller, sloppy housekeeping that makes a buyer feel uncomfortable, and areas in disrepair that raise questions of how well a home has been cared for.

The house was a perfect candidate. The interior was small—just 1,200 square feet—so any furnishings and accessories beyond a minimalist's style made it feel tiny and cramped. The owner's office was in her home, and office supplies and equipment were everywhere—the living room, dining room, even a hallway to the kitchen! A second bedroom contained three large exercise machines and an entertainment center that took up so much space one could barely step into the room; imagining it as a bedroom was a tall order. In fact, the house itself was so cluttered I had difficulty figuring out how the owner had room for her cat. Yet my trained eye could see that structurally the house was exquisite in every detail and had the potential to become an elegant home. I made several easy-to-execute suggestions for the homeseller to help buyers discover the potential of the house: move all the office equipment to the basement, creating a specific space for an office and demonstrating that the need for a home office did not equate giving up the house; remove all but one exercise machine from the second bedroom and add a love seat to help buyers envision alternative uses for the space. The owner made the changes and received three offers from four prospects on the first day!

Without these changes I am certain that one of two things would have happened: either several buyers would have passed it by before one arrived who could see through the clutter to the full potential, or the offers would have been far below the owner's asking price.

Cleanliness

When a house is unclean, it will make you feel uncomfortable, apprehensive, and hesitant about continuing the tour. Look for signs of whether the problem is just sloppy housekeeping or symptomatic of overall neglect. Laundry piled high, sinks and tubs that haven't seen cleanser in a month, walls and woodwork covered with fingerprints, or dirty floors and dingy windows may just be signs of a shoddy housekeeper. Of course, it's entirely reasonable to cut the tour short if you're disgusted and not willing to look further.

But it may well be worth your while to look *through* the current owner's mess. During the eight years in our blended family home, a house across the street sold three times. The house itself was a picturesque country-style cottage, complete with a picket fence and a perennial flower garden. The first owners sold in order to retire to the country, and the house was on the market for less than a week. The new owner, a single mother with two teenagers, snapped it up before the FOR SALE sign went in the yard. Several years later she remarried and moved out of state. The house had a lovely pool and backyard, but it went up for sale in the fall—not an ideal time in Minnesota to obtain the best price for a house with a pool. When her house didn't sell immediately, she decided to wait for the beauty of early summer and rented it to a group of young bachelors to avoid a double mortgage payment. These tenants' housekeeping habits had a definite negative effect on the house's salability. Few prospective buyers were able to see beyond the piles of laundry, stacks of dirty dishes, or whatever else may have lurked beneath the general disarray. The price dropped, but the house still sat on the market until a creative family was able to see a terrific bargain underneath the mess.

Transform drab and dirty into bright and spacious.

If the problems appear to be on the surface, imagine what a team of cleaners, painters, or even exterminators could do in a week. Just cleaning windows can shed a whole new light on a space! As a percentage of the purchase price, the cost of cleaning is very small. If you do the cleaning yourself, figure supplies to cost under $50. Professional housecleaners can cost $10 to $20 an hour, depending on your area. If the space doesn't look like it can be cleaned, a gallon of paint can go a long way. Paint costs vary, although you can figure $10 to $20 per gallon will result in a house that looks and feels like new! What's more, a thorough cleaning and a fresh coat of paint are an inspiring beginning and a great way for taking ownership.

If pets or smokers live in the house, you'll want to have the carpets professionally cleaned. Plan to spend up to $200 a room for professional carpet cleaners, or wait for specials (which seem to run nearly every month). Or check to see if hardwood floors are camouflaged by dated or worn carpet you can easily discard.

As gross as it may sound, even pests are not an unsurmountable problem. A pest inspection can be a contingency of a purchase agreement and provide you with an "out" if it reveals more extensive problems than surface nuisance. Extermination costs can vary from $100 or more for a onetime fumigation to several hundred dollars for an annual contract. Or you may be able to have the seller pay for services to make the house pest free.

Repair Versus Remodeling

A house that needs repair should send warning signals. Heed the signs before you sign; if there appear to be serious problems, beware. But if what looks like disrepair is actually routine maintenance, try to calculate realistically how much time and money will be involved. For example, if the faucet in the basement laundry tub is dripping, can it be fixed with a twenty-five-cent washer or is it a sign of a greater problem? Sellers are obligated to disclose any known defects, and in any case your purchase agreement should include a home inspection contingency (see page 125). You can also ask the seller to provide a homebuyers' warranty to ensure good working condition of major appliances and systems. Or you might want to purchase this insurance yourself to protect against unexpected repairs. If you're handy a home in need of minor maintenance may be a good buy. It should be priced less than comparable houses in top condition in the same area, and your sweat equity investment can pay off when you sell.

On the other hand, if your immediate response is to start moving walls or renovating a kitchen, remodeling requires looking at several factors. Will the project you undertake return your investment? The answer lies in the location, how long you plan to live in the house, and how much you spend. If the house is currently priced in the upper tier of the neighborhood, major renovation may put you in a difficult position when you sell. Buyers willing to pay your price will likely find a better investment in a neighborhood where a similarly priced house will appreciate more because it is in an area of higher-priced homes. However, if the listing price of the property reflects that it is outdated or at the lower end of the price range in a desirable neighborhood, consider the scope of any improvements and how they rank on the payback schedule for your area. These schedules vary by region and city. *Remodeling* magazine, available at the public library, publishes "Cost vs. Value" each year itemizing costs and resale impact for sixty cities in the East, South, Midwest, and West. The report tracks the cost of twelve prevalent remodeling projects and how much homeowners can expect to recover if they sell within a year of completing the project.

——— 🏠 ———

Will renovation renew your bottom line?

When looking at a house that has been extensively remodeled, for instance with an updated kitchen, bath, or a new addition, be aware that you're paying for it. It's very likely that some of the cost of the work has been added to the sale price of the home. If the remodeling is not exactly to your liking, you may be better off spending less for a house and remodeling it according to your own style. When we purchased our blended family home, we were enamored of an expensively remodeled master suite that included a freestanding marble fireplace, a hot tub, and a steam shower. We used the hot tub three times in eight years and built a fire twice. These features added ambience to the room but functionally didn't fit our busy lifestyle. However, the kitchen and deck were exceptional, having been remodeled in a fashion that would have been precluded by our budget. The trade-off was well worth it.

Design Features and Decorating Styles

Few buyers want to *start* with work, and you may decide to continue your search if a house isn't in move-in condition. However, if the seller hasn't been willing or financially able to make a house design-current or decorate it fashionably, you may be able to get a bargain if you have the time and inclination to invest in cosmetic changes.

Try to look at the "bones"—the basic structure and features—of a house, not the furniture, decorating, or how a room is being used. Before you say you don't like it, define "it." Is it the house itself, or is it someone else's decorating you find offensive? If the house fits your basic criteria, determine the extent of cosmetic changes that would be needed to reflect your style and taste. A room can be wallpapered in a weekend for a few hundred dollars, and carpeting can be replaced or torn up without borrowing from a 401(k). While these improvements seldom pay back at selling time, their contribution to your lifestyle and comfort level may be sufficient incentive if the house and neighborhood are a sound investment.

Dated ceramic tile is another common objection from buyers but a problem easily addressed through the use of complementary neutral colors. For example, in one of my houses dated pink and gray ceramic tile overpowered a small bathroom. Adding wallpaper with an ivory background and a gray-green ivy print with muted burgundy flowers converted the room from small and dated to

Today's dated feature may be tomorrow's trend.

quaint and charming for less than $50. For a client's house I recommended bright, crisp white linens and a fabric shower curtain in a bathroom with blue tile and pink trim. The transformation was stunning—the blue and white became dominant, and the pink gave the room an art deco look. Don't get side-tracked by a dated or unusual feature; with a little twist it might become something in vogue.

A House You Don't Like Is as Valuable as One You Do

Even houses that hold little appeal for you can provide useful insights for your search. If you know immediately that a house isn't for you, trust your intuition and cut the tour short. After you've left the house, be sure to articulate what you didn't like. Whether you're working with an agent or looking on your own, what you don't like can be a clue to choosing more appropriate houses for the next tour. For instance, an agent took a client to see a house that met all her must haves and she loved its looks, but the sounds from a nearby freeway were so disturbing she couldn't get past the living room. It was a clear lesson for the buyer—and her agent—that a quiet neighborhood was an essential element of her HomePrint.

Remember the couple who thought they wanted a duplex? They always found a similar problem with each house they toured—size. When looking at duplexes with two bedrooms, they contemplated how to add a third. In another that had three bedrooms, they thought the bedrooms were too small. Ultimately they came to real-ize the issue wasn't the houses but that they weren't ready to down-size or to share a dwelling. Jumping at the first single-family property they toured was a reaction to the discomfort they felt after having looked at so many duplexes and town houses. Consistent negative responses to homes that seem to meet your criteria may mean it's time to reevaluate your list.

If houses don't fit your criteria, maybe your criteria aren't fitting your needs.

If you haven't seen anything you like after looking at ten or more houses, the problem may be communication. Discuss your con-cerns with your agent to make sure that you have accurately identified what you want and that she clearly understands what you're looking for. If you still end up touring houses that aren't close to your list, and you are certain of your criteria, it may be time to look for another agent. We looked at *fifty* houses before finding one for our blended family. I know our agent felt that we were just being exceptionally choosy. In retrospect, I think he didn't understand the emotional element we were looking for in a house and couldn't identify it when he pretoured. He became frustrated and started showing us anything in the market with five bedrooms! We could have saved ourselves significant time had we found an agent with a better grasp of our objectives.

Avoiding Confusion

On the average homebuyers will look at twelve houses over an eight-week period. After seeing five or six houses, it's difficult to remember which one had which feature. Did the colonial have the red door, or was it the Cape Cod? Which one had the new gran-ite countertops? Often, as a matter of organization, buyers will link a house to a strong feature: "the house in the woods," the "die-for" patio, or the "one with orange shag carpeting." To maintain objectivity and sort through the confusion, start a file and record comparable information about each house you tour. This will enable you to compare notes more impartially after a long day of househunting, and to evaluate those truly outstanding features in context. If three of six houses are appealing and all have two-car garages and the third bathroom you want, then by all means go with the one with the great marble fireplace. It's an added bonus to meeting all your must haves.

Undistracted eyes see more.

A hint for families with small children: You'll find you're able to be a more relaxed, more objective "looker" when the tour group is limited. You can keep everyone's interests at heart without taking everyone on every tour. Children usually don't like being dragged from house to house and become easily distracted. Babies and toddlers demand attention and can distract you. While it is important to keep everyone involved, the final decision is yours. Save the family tours for when you've narrowed the search.

When your day of househunting is over, review the information on each house and make any additional notes and remarks on your Househunters' Notes. If you definitely decide against a house, remove it from the folder. (However, hold the information in a separate file until you've made your choice and are certain you won't want to review your notes.) If a house is still in the running, leave it in your folder so you can compare it with other houses on the next tour. Try to limit your favorites to three. If there are more than three, you might need to reevaluate your criteria to narrow your options.

When You Think You've Found the Right House ...

Reacting quickly and rationally will set the course for the next chapter in your life. It's at the point when you think you've found the right house that you'll be tempted to skip steps because you won't want to lose it. Take a breath, and before proceeding to an offer (or simultaneously if your market is hot), retrace your steps to stay in control at this very emotional time.

1. Compare the house to your HomePrint worksheets. How does it measure up to your objective list? If the house you are considering, whether it is one of the first you have seen or one of many, involves a compromise in location, style, or features, step back and evaluate how the compromise will affect your household and your lifestyle. Be exceptionally cautious if the concession you are considering is someone's top priority! If the location is questionable, consider the long-term financial impact, or compromises your family may need to make in commuting time or proximity to activities. Compromises are inevitable when buying a house; the key is to be aware of their long-term impact.

2. Walk through the house again.

   - Pay close attention to the floor plan and traffic patterns and how they will affect daily living. Will routine chores such as laundry and preparing meals be efficient? What will mornings be like when the household is getting ready for work or school?

   - Bring a tape measure and go through every room. Imagine how your furniture will fit. If you have a prized piece, measure it in the room it's in now and compare it with where it might be placed. A good friend of mine had to put an antique bed in storage because it wouldn't fit through a hallway. In my last house I couldn't get a queen-size mattress up the stairs and had to have a carpenter cut space in a hallway.

- Make a list of everything you want to include in the purchase agreement: draperies, light fixtures, and appliances. You might want to take photos to help you remember these details.

- If the seller happens to be at home during a tour, make sure you refrain from any conversation—positive or negative—about the house. If you don't like a feature, the seller may be offended and be less responsive to an offer. If you love the house and are bubbling over with the excitement of making an offer, the seller may be less likely to negotiate, knowing your heart is set on the house.

- Three times is plenty. If you have to go back more than that, look at what's bothering you.

3. Confirm the location.

- Go back to the neighborhood at different times of day. The street that wasn't so busy at two o'clock on a Sunday afternoon may become an expressway during rush hour.

- Make the drive to work. Is the twenty-minute commute that was advertised to your office door or to the edge of the city? How far is the house from the activities that are important to you: schools, athletics, hobbies, cultural attractions, your social activities, shopping?

- Walk through the neighborhood. What does it feel like? Houses look different when you're walking than when you're driving. Don't be afraid to knock on doors and talk to neighbors. One spring a woman rang my doorbell and asked if she could talk about the neighborhood and the highway that ran behind our house and the one she was considering. I was quite surprised at first but relished the chance to talk about my neighborhood and share "insider" knowledge. I explained that any noise was negligible because the highway was asphalt rather than concrete and the sound wall provided further insulation. I went on to talk about the family orientation of the neighbors and activities we enjoyed through the neighborhood association. She and her family purchased the house and found the neighborhood to be exactly what they wanted. Refer again to the checklist "Preapprove Your Neighborhood" on page 48.

● Go to the grocery store. One woman told me of looking for a home to reflect her husband's business stature. They found a house that seemed perfect, but when she stopped in the grocery store, she realized that the other customers weren't whom she had envisioned for neighbors. A bit snooty, but true to what she wanted.

4. Reevaluate your financial investment.

● Check the real estate environment in the immediate neighborhood. What are the selling and pricing trends, owner-versus-rental ratio, crime statistics, environmental issues, future zoning changes, construction, corporate activity?

   If the signs are positive, you'll feel confident knowing the house you love will likely be a sound financial investment. If the answers don't point in the right direction and you can't afford the risk, think about another house. If you find yourself saying, "I don't care, I love the house," it's time to step back. Consider realistically what you are willing to overlook to buy this house: what is the risk?

● If you are already thinking about remodeling, check where the house falls in the price range of the neighborhood. If your plans will put you at the top, you may have a more difficult time selling. A relative of mine insisted on purchasing a home in a specific neighborhood. He bought the first house available and didn't care that the floor plan wasn't what he wanted. The school district was great, and the athletic program was right for his two young sons. He started remodeling as soon as he moved in, and his house has been in disarray for four years! Meanwhile, over a dozen houses in his neighborhood have sold. He might have saved a substantial amount of money by waiting for the right *house* in the right neighborhood. He is now ready to sell again and wonders if he can recoup the extensive remodeling costs.

You're almost home. Your preparation has helped you stay in control of the flurry of options and possibilities around you and paved the way for the final step, actually purchasing your home. You can proceed confidently, knowing you've balanced a multifaceted decision and weighed the effect it will have on the well-being of your household *and* your financial situation.

Househunters' Notes

Making thorough notes on the houses you tour will enable you to compare them objectively when you're ready to make a decision. Evaluate each feature on a scale of 1 to 5, 5 being outstanding. Make notes or take photos. Then add up the points to see how each house measures up to your HomePrint priorities.

Total score: _____

Overall ranking to date: _____

General

Address: _____

Year built: _____   Financing: _____

Price: $_____   Taxes: $ _____

Utility costs: _____   Possession date: _____

Lot size: _____   Style: _____

(add a photo and attach listing sheet)

First Impressions

General exterior condition: _____

Neighborhood: _____

General interior condition: _____

Location/Neighborhood

Distance from work: _____   Commuting time: _____

Transportation: _____

Schools: _____

   Student-teacher ratio: _____

   Expenditure per student: _____

   Test ranking: _____

   Special programs/activities: _____

Shopping and conveniences: _____

Cultural activities: _____

Appearance of homes: _____

Age mix of residents: _____

Community/neighborhood organization: _____

Traffic patterns: _____

Zoning: _____

Crime statistics: _____

Other: _____

Rank 1–5

Physical Structure

Number of bedrooms: _____   _____

Number of baths: _____   _____

Kitchen: size, type: _____   _____

Dining room/space: _____   _____

Entertaining space: _____   _____

Family room/great room: _____   _____

Living room: _____   _____

Home office: _____   _____

Other main rooms: _____   _____

Practicality of floor plan: _____   _____

Natural light: _____   _____

Condition:

    Carpet/floors: _____   _____

    Paint: _____   _____

    Stairs: _____   _____

    Windows: _____   _____

    Decorating: _____   _____

    Plumbing/heating/electrical/air: _____   _____

Basement: _____   _____

Hobby space: _____   _____

Garage: _____   _____

Storage spaces: _____   _____

Items included or excluded:

_____

_____

_____

                                                    Rank 1–5
Exterior
Curb appeal: _____   _____
Yard: _____   _____
   Garden space: _____   _____
   Landscaping: _____   _____
   Play space, entertaining space: _____   _____
Roof: _____   _____
Foundation: _____   _____
Driveway/sidewalks: _____   _____
Deck, patio, or pool: _____   _____
View: _____   _____
Other: _____   _____

Environment
Water: public, well: _____
Waste disposal: _____
Recycling availability: _____
Other: _____

Resale Potential
Where is this house in the price range of the neighborhood now? What
are the prices and selling times of comparable homes for sale in this
area?

_____

_____

_____

What is the pricing trend (increasing or decreasing)? _____

_____

Are any zoning changes or construction proposed that could affect the
neighborhood?_____

_____

_____

Which of our Top Five Features does this house have?

_____

_____

_____

_____

_____

Notes/Sketches

CHAPTER 6

Step Four:
The Art of the Deal

When you're almost home, the combination of your excitement and your lack of familiarity with legalese can hinder attending to all the details involved in this stage: the terms of an offer, contingencies, counteroffers, inspections, mortgage documentation, appraisal, and closing. In the midst of life itself, the process can feel unmanageable. Even the most seasoned homebuyer can be tempted to eliminate steps when everything *appears* to be in order. Remember the couple who decided against a home inspection just because they couldn't handle one more detail? As a result they had one more detail anyway: the bats. A potential disaster would have occurred to the couple who had bought a dozen houses if their agent hadn't insisted on the inspection that uncovered the missing support beam.

If you've done your homework, you'll have your resources in place: a real estate agent, a mortgage lender, a home inspector, a real estate attorney, and an insurance agent. You made the decision to rely on professionals *before* the passion of a house entered the picture. Trust your judgment from that more objective period and stick to your plan. You can still shop around for services, but think twice about skipping any steps or deciding that "good enough" will do. If you find yourself making decisions without fully understanding your options, or thinking, I'm sure it's fine, take a breath and refocus. It's at this stage you'll truly appreciate a relationship with a good real estate agent, who will take charge and handle many of the details. If you're managing the process yourself, rely on your plan and trust the judgments of the service professionals you've engaged. After all, why pay for advice you'll ignore?

The details of completing a real estate transaction vary widely by state and region and change frequently. However, the basics apply to most purchases. In general, make sure you understand everything before you sign. A real estate document is binding, so if you have questions, don't hesitate to voice them or seek professional guidance. As at odds as it may seem with the magnitude of the purchase of a house, there are hundreds of hindsight stories from buyers who have blindly accepted every document because they didn't want to *appear* unknowledgeable or who became overwhelmed with the size of the financial commitment and dug their heels in at the thought of spending one more dollar. Think twice about forgoing professional advice for the sake of saving a few hundred dollars. The peace of mind alone may be worth the investment.

Keeping this important warning in mind, you're now ready to enter the process of purchasing your house. While each transaction varies, the process involves just three stages. First, making an offer includes deciding price, contingencies, and other conditions. Once the seller accepts your offer, you have a contract. (In some states the offer is submitted on a purchase agreement, which becomes the contract. This is how I'll refer to it in this chapter. In other states a separate document is used to make the offer, and when it is accepted you "go to contract" and the legalese is added.) In the second stage you'll complete your financ-

Click your heels—you're almost home.

ing, have the house appraised, and secure your insurance. The final stage, the closing, completes the purchase: the seller receives payment, and you have a house! How smooth your sailing is will be directly related to how well you have done your homework.

Making an Offer

Deciding how much to offer and negotiating is more of an art than a science. Because the real estate market is always changing, there is no exact formula to help you arrive at the magic number. On the average, houses sell for 5 to 6 percent less than the asking price. But averages are only averages and may not be specific to your market at your time. Houses sell close to, or even above, asking prices in a sellers' market (when there are fewer houses for sale than buyers); they sell for less when there are more houses than buyers. Educated buyers will be aware of the market and what a house will sell for. Working with a good agent will give you insight into the local market and how "well" a house is priced, as well as a keen perspective on its resale potential. In any market several objective factors will come into play when arriving at an offer:

> The market and the house offer clues to a solid offer.

- How a property stacks up to the competition will give you a realistic idea of how much it is worth. Looking at comparable selling prices—"comps"—will show you what similar houses in the neighborhood have sold for. This information will suggest what percentage of the listing price the sellers may be expecting. If you don't have an agent, you might want to consider hiring one at this stage. He'll have access to information on past and recent comparable selling prices for similar properties in the neighborhood. *Recent* is key, because it will give you an accurate picture of the current market.

- The condition of a property will be reflected in the selling price. A house in move-in condition will sell at the top of its range, while one needing repairs will sell for less, depending on the extent of the work required. Chances are that the owners of a "fixer upper" will have placed it on the market knowing it will bring a lower price. If repairs are needed, you'll want to consider their true cost when making an offer. If repairs cost less than you think, you'll feel better about the house; if the cost of necessary repairs is beyond your expectations, determine whether a bargain on the house is worth the strain on your budget. More important, calculate the return on your investment. If the house is in need of repair, recognize that when it comes time to sell, a savvy buyer, just like you, will not expect to pay top dollar for a house in less than top condition. Does the resale potential of the house bear the cost of the repairs? Looking at the selling prices of similar houses in good repair can help you determine how much leeway you have. A home inspection (see page 90) is your best insurance when making an offer on a house in need of work. Including it as a contingency will give you options *after* making an offer.

—— 🏠 ——

Guesstimates are no substitute for estimates.

- The reasons for selling a house can also help you strategically calculate a price to offer. Your agent may be able to ascertain the reasons the house is for sale, or you can ask neighbors. A client of mine always makes a point to stop and talk to children in the neighborhood. Their answers can provide information worth checking out.

    Owners of houses that are on the market because of a corporate relocation may be open to lower offers. In many cases the employer will have guaranteed a certain price to the owners or even purchased the house from them as a condition of the transfer. In job transfer situations, companies are concerned with the bottom line and may consider a lesser offer if it includes a quick closing date because that will reduce their "holding" costs.

- The time a listing has been on the market will also affect how much, if any, the owners will be willing to negotiate. You'll have less flexibility with a new listing than with one that's been on the market for several months.

When you have all the facts together, deciding how much to offer will be clearer. Remember, a little bargaining is expected, although if the information you have shows that the house is well priced, don't risk submitting a lowball offer thinking the sellers will counter with their bottom-end price. You may end up offending the sellers and having them accept another, more realistic bid.

Houses in a hot market may sell over list price. I recently talked with several agents in the midst of an exceptionally hot market on the West Coast. I asked what it was like to present offers in a market where houses sell in a heartbeat. Was it fun and exciting? I was quite surprised when they unanimously responded, "No!" They said it was not uncommon to receive five or six offers on a house, which meant that working with buyers and arriving at an offer was a matter more of playing a bidding game than of being able to help a buyer get a fair price. If you find yourself in a bidding war and aren't absolutely in love with the house, consider letting it go. You're going to pay top dollar—or more—which means the house may not appreciate as quickly. If you have the time to wait for another house, doing so may be wiser over the long term.

By all means, if you think you've found the right house at the right price, don't hesitate to make a strong offer—near, at, or even *over* listing price if it is especially attractive or priced right on the money and might be subject to multiple offers. Consult with your agent or attorney for conditions other than price that might make your offer more attractive. Will a quick closing be of value to the owner? Are there other terms of the sale that can position your offer better? Sellers can accept, reject, or counter your offer, so the stronger the offer, the better your chance of reaching an agreement.

> The goal of a real estate transaction is for seller *and* buyer to receive a fair price.

Your offer will also include an "earnest money" deposit, or binder, which demonstrates to the seller that you are serious about purchasing this house. The amount is typically 2 to 5 percent of the purchase price, depending on the asking price and your market. If your offer is accepted, the earnest money becomes part of the down payment. (If it is rejected and you don't reach an agreement, your earnest money will be returned.) Make a copy of the check. You'll need it to complete your mortgage application and again at closing.

In addition to price and terms of payment, a purchase agreement contains dozens of terms and conditions. Here are some basics:

- **Acceptance time.** A seller generally has one or two days to accept the offer. Any longer is an invitation to the seller to wait for a better offer. If you're in a hot market, consider providing an incentive to respond quickly and positively. When my daughter was making an offer on a house, the agent tied the purchase price to the acceptance time: the offer was for full price *if* accepted by midnight of the day it was presented. Otherwise, the offer was 6 percent less.
- **Personal property.** The rule on personal property is this: If it's attached to the house, it stays. You may want to add specific items, such as draperies, wall unit air conditioners, or appliances to your purchase agreement. However, if you want to

purchase furniture or equipment—for example, pool cleaning tools, barbecues, lawn furniture, or even a satellite dish—negotiate with the seller and document your deal in a separate agreement. If a seller has specifically excluded an item (an antique chandelier, for example), make certain it will be replaced with a fixture you approve. Specify a price or a fixture of your choosing. You may want to take a photo of the existing item to compare it with the replacement.

- **Contingencies.** A variety of safeguards can be included in your offer. How many and what you include will depend on the house and your market. In a sellers' market an offer with multiple contingencies may be rejected; if a property has been on the market for a long time, the sellers may be more open to contingencies.

  - Every agreement should be subject to—or contingent on —obtaining financing from a lender of your choice, even if you are preapproved. The purchase agreement will specify a time limit for you to make application for a loan.

  - Include a contingency for a home inspection by an inspector of your choice. Most standard home inspection contingency clauses give the buyer ten days to obtain an inspection, but you can designate any time you wish. While you bear the costs of an inspection, you may want to include language that states if any repairs made by the seller are not to your satisfaction, you may cancel the contract or reduce the price of the house to cover repair costs. You might also include that if repairs made do not pass a reinspection, the cost of any future inspections will be borne by the seller.

  - If you have a home to sell before you buy another, you'll want a contingency providing for the sale so you don't end up with more than one mortgage. Such contingencies will state that the seller must notify you when and if another offer is received. You'll then have a specified amount of time, generally forty-eight hours, to remove the contingency or terminate the agreement. In a strong real estate market, don't be surprised if a seller doesn't agree to this contingency. Positioning your current house for a fast sale is the best insurance you have that you won't be faced with the decision to remove a contingency and risk multiple mortgage payments, or to give up a house you love.

- A pest inspection can ensure you won't be sharing your home with unwanted tenants. While the bat infestation in one couple's attic space may have been visible to a home inspector, smaller pests such as termites leave signs only a trained eye can detect, so a separate pest inspection is wise.

- Consider a homebuyers' warranty plan to protect you against problems with the plumbing, heating, cooling, and electrical systems. The seller usually picks up the tab on such a warranty.

- **Closing date.** This date is dependent on when you want to take possession of the house, the seller's situation, and the time needed to obtain a mortgage. Check with your lender in advance to see how long you should allow. A safe guideline is six weeks, although the industry is working to speed up the process. (Here is another reason why obtaining a mortgage preapproval is a smart move—it can take weeks off the closing date.)

- **Possession date.** Occupancy usually occurs within a day of closing.

- **Walkthrough.** This is a provision for a final tour, generally on the day of closing, to make certain that the house is in the same condition as when the seller accepted your offer.

- **Lead paint addendum.** The Environmental Protection Agency requires that the seller of a house built before 1978 give the buyer ten days to conduct an inspection for lead paint hazards.

You may change the timing, and you may elect to delete the addendum. If hazards are found a seller cannot be required to remedy the flaw, but you are not obligated to complete the purchase.

Discuss the other conditions in your purchase agreement with your agent or attorney, and be certain you understand the implication of each. You may add contingencies you feel appropriate to the house and any concerns you may have. You may wish to ask the seller to complete your own Property Information Sheet (see Appendix I). It is more comprehensive than the standard disclosures in a purchase agreement. While it is not a warranty, this questionnaire will provide more detailed information on the house, its systems, and its surroundings.

Although an offer is just an offer until it is accepted, once a seller accepts your offer, the agreement is binding, so you may wish to have a real estate attorney review the agreement before submitting it.

The offer will usually be presented by your agent. Because objectivity is a fundamental of good negotiation, you don't want to go along. (Believe me, you won't be objective.) The seller may accept, reject, or return the volley and counter your offer. Once countered you can agree to the new terms or counter the counteroffer. Every time you counter it means you reject the other offer and the seller can stop playing the game, so be reasonable. I've known of many sellers who have stopped the process just on "principle"—I've done it myself. Because an offer can include everything from appliances to closing costs, you may find yourself bargaining over more than price. This is where skilled negotiation plays a key role.

Making an offer and responding to counteroffers can be very

Objectivity is the key to negotiation.

emotional and fast paced—it's not unusual to see a house and make an offer in a matter of hours. If you've read the purchase agreement, understand the market, and know what constitutes legitimate contingencies for both the house *and* the market, you will feel more in control of all the decisions to be made and more confident that the offer you are making is thorough.

When the offer is accepted and you have a contract, activity goes into high gear to ensure that all the details and time limits are attended to. Now is when your preparation will pay off in a big way. Imagine the pressure of having to interview and select a lender, a home inspector, and an insurance agent within a few short days. It's no wonder that unprepared buyers can find this period agonizing. *You* can almost begin packing!

Finalizing the Financing

If you have obtained preapproval, you or your agent will deliver copies of the purchase agreement and earnest money check to your lender.

This is the most common time to "lock in" your interest rate. You will also select a title insurance company or escrow company, which will coordinate the closing. Your lender, agent, or attorney can recommend one, or you can shop for one yourself. The costs don't vary greatly, but you'll want to be sure the company is well established if you decide to shop.

The appraisal fee will be due before the lender orders the appraisal, which can take a week or two, depending on the market. Review the revised good faith estimate of closing costs, and make certain you understand every cost required. You'll also receive an Initial Truth in Lending Disclosure Statement, which is an estimate of your loan costs. When the house has been appraised at an amount that covers the lender's exposure, or risk, you'll be

Buyer's Remorse

Sometime shortly after your offer is accepted, you may find yourself questioning your decision. This is a normal adult reaction to the stress of change and the size of the financial commitment. It happens to almost all people who purchase houses, regardless of how many times they have been through the process. Some remedies for this homebuying phenomenon include the following:

- Review your HomePrint, Househunters' Notes, and all the reasons you chose this house.
- Be assured that lenders are conservative. If you weren't qualified to repay the loan, you would have been denied a mortgage. If the house wasn't worth the mortgage, you'd have known that, too.
- If you must, tour the house again. If you really want to back out, determine the financial ramifications and then sleep on it.

After we purchased our blended family home, the sellers invited us for an afternoon pool party. I hadn't taken two steps into the house when I experienced a severe case of buyer's remorse. I felt nauseated and overcome with dread. The house was in the suburbs. I love the city. The house was a remodeled 1950s rambler. I love older houses with interesting spaces. My husband calmly reminded me of all the reasons we chose the house, and my children repeatedly reassured me that it was a good choice. It took days, but the condition passed.

notified of loan approval, and it will be time to start packing! (Be sure to request a copy of your appraisal after the closing.)

If you haven't received preapproval, you'll need to begin the mortgage application process immediately. The steps are the same as those outlined on page 85: once you select a lender and your application is complete, processing begins. Written verification of employment, assets, and debts will be requested and an appraisal will be ordered. When all the documentation has been received, the lender will evaluate the application. Expect processing of the application to take six weeks or more.

Loans get delayed for any number of reasons. Lenders are processing a record number of loans, which means requests for written verifications from credit card companies and financial institutions increase. Documentation can be lost or misplaced. If your schedule is tight, you may become impatient. Don't wait for a month to check on the progress of the loan. You don't have to be a pest, but your call may draw attention to a missing item that would otherwise go undetected for some time.

Frequent checkups keep a loan on track.

Ordering Your Home Inspection

Your purchase agreement will specify a period in which you have to obtain a home inspection. As soon as your offer is accepted, notify your inspector of the time restrictions and set a date to accompany him to the house. Be sure you take notes, thoroughly discuss his comments, and obtain a specific written report rather than a standard printout. When you receive the report, read it thoroughly. If you are not certain about an item, seek additional advice before accepting the report. When an inspector noted that it "appeared" that the mortar in our chimney was breaking down, we called a chimney repair service to verify the extent of the problem. If the report uncovers defects, discuss them with your agent and determine how they can best be remedied according to your contract. If negotiation is required, again, try to stay out of the discussions.

Remember, *no* house is perfect.

If you're hesitating about spending the money on a home inspector, remember the story of the missing support beam. You can be assured that the few hundred dollars for a home inspection was less than the repair cost.

Finalizing Your Insurance

While your mortgage is being processed, contact your insurance agent to purchase a homeowners' policy. Review the options available (see page 92) and select a policy that protects your investment and your household. The lender will require proof of homeowners' insurance at the closing, and your insurance agent will provide a binder. You'll likely have to prepay a portion of the premium.

If you put down less than 20 percent and end up having to carry private mortgage insurance, it will be your responsibility to notify the mortgage company when you have reached the 20 percent equity necessary to terminate the insurance. Keep an eye on your neighborhood and what similar houses are selling for. When you're comfortable that your equity is adequate, obtain an appraisal on your house to verify that your mortgage balance is less than 80 percent of the appraised value of the house. A good, ongoing relationship with your real estate agent can help. He or she can run a competitive market analysis at no cost to monitor when spending the money on an appraisal is warranted.

The Closing

This is the step that finally makes *the* house *your* house. It involves transferring the ownership from the seller to you—but not until you sign a bizillion documents!

A few days before the closing, set a specific time for your final walkthrough to make certain that the house is in the same condition as when the offer was accepted. Be sure to bring any photos and notes for comparison. Your agent and often the seller will be present. Take your time and walk carefully through the house, checking to ensure that it has been well maintained, that no damage has occurred and no items are missing. If you see a problem, now is the time to bring it up and agree—in writing—on a resolution.

Avoid aftershock with a thorough walkthrough.

If you are closing on the house you are selling and the one you are buying on the same day, coordinate the closings to avoid overlap and delay. In many states and areas the parties sign documents separately and the title is transferred without a formal meeting. In other states both parties attend the meeting and sign documents, and the players can include closers, attorneys, and more.

Every agent and lender has war stories to tell about closings that have been delayed or have taken hours—even days—to complete. In all my closings I have never experienced any delays. Keeping in touch with your lender, your agent, and your title insurance or escrow company will keep everything on track. If you have any questions, you can resolve them before the closing. Review your estimate of closing costs and verify the amounts with your lender so you arrive prepared. Then when you arrive your only concern will be writer's cramp.

Don't underestimate the emotional impact of the closing—the purchase of a house is a momentous occasion. If you can, take the day off, or try not to schedule yourself tightly that day. If delays occur you won't need the added stress of juggling personal meetings or child care arrangements. If you have a mature child consider having him or her attend the closing. Although children will likely declare such an opportunity "boring," it will help their understanding of the magnitude of the purchase. And while this may be the biggest day of your life, recognize that it is routine for most people at the meeting. Don't be offended if those around you don't seem to be as moved by the occasion as you are. It's not a housewarming party—although I've seen some spectacular closing gifts.

Congratulations...

You're the proud owner of a new house. You've discovered that finding home can be a rewarding life adventure and isn't as complicated or fraught with pitfalls as the cynics would have you believe. Whether you've just paid hundreds of thousands of dollars for a home or have uncovered a gem for a fraction of that price, the feeling of accomplishment is the same. It is a new beginning—a fresh start—for you and your household. It brings with it an exhilarating feeling of anticipation. Savor the moment for as long as you can before racing back to finish packing or hustling to your new house to direct the movers.

CHAPTER 7

This End Up!

A Guide to Moving with More Fun and Less Hassle

In many ways our last move was similar to leaving the storybook family house where you brought your children home, raised them, and waved good-bye when they went off to college. While we lived in our house for only eight years, it is the house our blended family thinks of as our first. The backyard was the scene of a wedding reception, a baby shower, three high school graduation parties, family reunions, falling-down-laughter croquet games, and countless dinners and get-togethers with friends and neighbors. There will always be a place in my heart for the intimate family memories attached to that house. I can fully understand why some homeowners choose to stay put during the empty-nest years, and once grandchildren arrive, they don't think of moving as a choice.

We were determined to balance the excitement and adventure of moving to an older house in the city with the emotional facet of saying good-bye to comfortable places and familiar faces. When scheduling the details of our move, we took care to include time for one last backyard event and one last gazebo get-together with our next-door neighbors.

Nonetheless, there were nostalgic and sentimental periods when I wondered if we'd made the right choice. The mixed emotions began with the decision to sell the house and continued throughout the selling, buying, and moving process. The week before moving day, while I was busy packing in the kitchen, I was surprised to hear my twelve-year-old stepson, who usually walked the family dog begrudgingly, "ask" him if he wanted to go for a walk to say good-bye to the neighborhood pets. The somewhat joking "conversation" continued with questions to the dog that revealed his own trepidations: "So, Benson, are you feeling sad about leaving your house? Do you wonder if there will be any dogs in our new neighborhood?"

Although my stepson was thrilled about the new house, especially his third-floor "suite," he too was experiencing the mixture of emotions surrounding the move. That afternoon my husband helped him produce a real "home" movie—a videotape of the house and the neighborhood. It seemed to make the finality of the move less traumatic, and the fun of the activity balanced the anxiety.

The next week, after the moving truck was packed and headed to our new house, my stepson and I went back for one last moment in this house that had brought two families together and held so many memories. He went upstairs to his room, and I stood alone for several minutes in the family room, where I was lost in a humorous memory when the new owners arrived. I turned to greet them with a smile amidst tears streaming down my face! My stepson had quietly left the house to wait for me in the car, and I found him with his arm around his dog friend and feeling as sad as I.

If you're like most people, you're probably wishing you could just go to bed one night and wake up the next morning in your new house with everything in its place. Whether your move is across the country or across town, the mere thought of packing and unpacking, the myriad details, and the weeks of disarray may be enough to make you want to swear off moving forever.

Moving is much more than the task-oriented process of packing, arranging for movers, and unpacking. It is also a psychological process that begins with your first discussion of moving and will continue even after you have settled into a new home, neighborhood, and routine. Taking the time to understand the mixture of emotions and the needs of everyone in the household can make farewells less bitter and more sweet, and getting settled easier and more rewarding. Savoring the memories of your house and all it has held for you will provide a meaningful send-off for the entire household.

This End Up! is an organized three-step program to help you balance the moving process just as the Finding Home approach to homebuying helped make certain the house you purchased was both a sound life and a sound financial investment. The program will put you in control of this last stage before you cross the threshold of your new home. This End Up! is complete with a schedule you can adapt to your lifestyle and time line and offers proven techniques for bringing order to chaos. By using it you'll be organized as never before and have more time to spend on the stuff of which memories are made—like taking a longer lunch with old friends, going for one last walk with your neighbor, or playing one more game of catch in the yard. The plan will introduce you to ideas that will help you gather and save your happy memories. You won't spend six weeks wishing you weren't moving, and when you arrive at your new house, you won't be left wondering *which* end is up.

> You can't move by waving a wand, but it can be as easy as 1-2-3!

Step One: Organizing and Scheduling

The time to organize your move is while you're waiting for the mortgage paperwork to clear. Start by reviewing the tasks and suggestions here and in the This End Up! Checklist on page 151. This program is based on a six-week plan of what to do and when to do it. Select what is appropriate for your own move and "back schedule" from your closing date. When you schedule backwards from the closing date, you'll begin to  see which steps overlap and where you'll need help. Create your own week-by-week master list, or work directly from the checklist.

If you don't have a full six weeks, tailor your list to fit your time frame. Be realistic. Don't try to crowd too much into one day or week, and don't try to do it all yourself. Ask for help from friends, neighbors, and relatives. Hire help for cleaning, hauling, and, of course, the move itself.

Get ahead of the game by reserving a truck or movers now if you'll be doing the moving on your own. If you are moving long distance and plan to use a professional moving company, schedule your moving estimates *after* the sorting process. You'll receive a lower estimate if the house is clear of excess items.

Marking Your Calendar

Gather everyone in your household and review the tasks and activities for the coming weeks. Asking for input and suggestions now will encourage everyone to help and to feel a part of the process rather than watch from the sidelines. Regular meetings will keep the move on track, head off potential problems, and develop a sense of teamwork.

Consider each family member's talents and abilities and what each enjoys doing, then assign appropriate tasks. For example, younger children can help by sorting their toys and returning borrowed items to neighbors.

Once you've made your schedule, transfer the list of tasks to a calendar and keep it posted for the whole household to follow. At the end of each week, or after an intense day of sorting or packing, tick

_____ 🏠 _____

Involving everyone makes for a smooth move.

off each completed item. This is a great way to keep the bigger picture in focus by highlighting how much has been accomplished while clearly showing what's left to be done—or what was missed!

Add an element of fun by scheduling rewards along the way, such as a night at the movies when the sorting step is complete. You can keep younger children focused with incentives for completing each task on time—reading an extra book at bedtime, renting a movie, having dinner at a favorite restaurant, or accumulating points toward the purchase of a special toy.

Making the Calls

The administrative details—coordinating everything from transferring doctor and dental records to changing your address and bank accounts—can be accomplished by following the timing guidelines from the This End Up! Checklist. If your move is imminent, your calls may need to be made earlier or divided among family members for efficiency. Home service companies and moving coordinators are an emerging service. If you're pressed for time, check with your agent or the yellow pages to see if these services are available in your area.

Running Errands

From returning library books and borrowed tools to taking pets to the vet and picking up dry cleaning, the running around before a move can take up valuable time. To make these chores less time intensive, consolidate errands by location and schedule trips during less busy traffic and shopping hours. Make a list of what needs to be accomplished and *delegate*!

Step Two: Sorting and Cleaning

The most important step in an organized move is sorting—going through all your belongings, returning items to their proper places, recycling unused items, or throwing away broken or damaged toys, appliances, and more. Putting everything in its place now will mean less chaos during packing and more organized unpacking in your new house. Whether you're doing it yourself or a moving company is packing for you, you'll feel the benefits of sorting long after the last box is unpacked.

Start by designating three "holding" places:

- A small basket, box, or tote for items and parts that belong elsewhere in the house.

- A larger box or area of your house for items you want to sell or donate, or need to return to neighbors or friends.

- A staging area for storing packed boxes. Stacking boxes in the garage makes for a less cluttered house during the process and easier loading on moving day.

Next, assemble an organizing and cleaning kit (a gardener's tote with compartments is ideal) with supplies and tools. Assembling supplies once will save time and make it easy to pick up the task where you left off or when you have a few unexpected moments to spare. Include these items in your tote:

- ☐ Small bucket
- ☐ Glass cleaner
- ☐ Cleanser
- ☐ All-purpose cleaner
- ☐ Furniture polish
- ☐ Paper towels
- ☐ Sponges
- ☐ Screwdrivers and pliers
- ☐ Tape measure
- ☐ Notepad and pen—to jot down items you need or ideas for your new house

- ☐ Garbage bags
- ☐ Small plastic zipper-lock bags
- ☐ Masking tape
- ☐ Self-adhesive file folder labels
- ☐ Hand vacuum

Go through your house room by room, moving to the next room only when every drawer, closet, and space in the last has been sorted and cleaned. Beware of the "clean sweep" and the tendency to discard too much. Make certain children are involved in this stage, and be sensitive to the items that others have chosen to save.

To sort a room, begin with the closet and built-ins, then move on to the drawers of furniture. First, remove everything. Evaluate

——— ♦ ———

Sort it out!

what you want to keep, what can be sold or donated, and what needs to be returned to a friend or neighbor. Consolidate bottles and boxes of identical items: food, baking supplies, cleaning supplies, and toiletries. Clean every container, wash knickknacks, and dust books. The result will be a fresh, clean feeling when you move. Imagine how pleasant unpacking toiletries in your new bathroom will be when everything is sparkling clean and there are no half-full bottles. It's like starting brand new!

Before replacing items, clean drawers and closets to save time on moving day. If you plan to hire a cleaning service to clean after you leave, focus on cleaning drawers and furniture that will go with you. When replacing articles, group like items together for more organized packing and unpacking. Neatly fold and stack linens, use small plastic containers or zipper-lock plastic bags for smaller items that could be easily lost.

When a room is complete, make one trip around the house to

return items and parts to their proper places before beginning the next room.

If you are on a tight schedule, you may need to start packing at this time. If not, resist the temptation. Packing will be more organized if you wait until you have sorted every room.

Savoring—and Saving—Your Memories

Don't be surprised if you get sidetracked when sorting. You may find yourself sitting in the middle of a room poring over old photo albums and memorabilia. Finding the last note my son had written to Santa was one of the most heartrending moments of my last move.

If you don't already have special keepsake boxes, now is a perfect time to create a "memory box" for each person. Any sturdy box will do, although I prefer to use a hard plastic box with a lid (a Rubbermaid tote is perfect), which will withstand the wear and tear of moving more than once. Create a decorative memory box label with markers or design a label on your computer (see Appendix II for a sample).

Take a trip down memory lane.

I first started making memory boxes with my children when they were finding it difficult to sort through school papers and the countless childhood articles and souvenirs they had accumulated over the years. Instead of the disheartening task of choosing what to throw or give away, deciding what to take to the new house and save forever became a positive undertaking. Of course, there is no age limit on memories, and what started as a project for kids became a family tradition. Now everyone in our household has a memory box. It's like having a scrapbook without the work of assembling it! Memory boxes provide a link to old spaces, places, and friends. They are guaranteed to rekindle sweet memories for years to come.

The Profitable Garage Sale

As you sort, you'll uncover a plethora of posses-sions that can be turned into cash. Everything from clothing and toys to furniture and appli-ances can add up to big money. With the right publicity and creative merchandising, you can turn your garage into a store for a day.

Publicity

- Use a descriptive headline in your ad that conveys merchandise quality.
- Pay a little extra for a larger ad, and list some of your better items.
- Call it a "moving sale," and schedule it on Saturday to attract more customers.
- Enlarge your ad on colored paper and place flyers in local stores. Distribute flyers to your neighbors, too.
- Purchase professional signs with bold arrows to attract customers.
- Hold a presale party for neighbors the night before your sale. You'll have more time to visit when you aren't in the thick of negotiating and selling—and they'll love the "first crack" opportunity.

Merchandising and Selling

- More is better. Invite neighbors to hold sales at the same time, or ask friends to bring items to sell at your sale.
- Make sure all items are sparkling clean and look appealing. Place blankets in clear plastic; tie linen sets together with raffia.

- Test all appliances and equipment to make certain they are in working condition. Have a power cord available on sale day so customers can test electrical items.
- Price items to sell, give discounts for multiple purchases, and be prepared to bargain. A fundamental of pricing is objectivity. Remember, if you've decided to sell it, you don't need it. It may be in good condition, but it is used. Garage salers are bargain hunters and don't expect to pay department store prices.
- Rent or borrow plenty of tables. Set up your merchandise two days before your sale if possible.
- Cover tables with decorative cloths, and arrange merchandise to encourage browsing. Keep household goods, toys, and clothing separate. Don't stack items or place them on the lawn.
- Create a "kids' stuff" table for young shoppers, and price it for young budgets.
- Order box lunches and have snacks on hand for workers.
- Purchase matching T-shirts and visors for workers.
- Place larger items in front to encourage traffic to stop.
- Use flags, streamers, and balloons to add an air of festivity.
- Have children tend a coffee or lemonade and cookie stand.
- Set up a checkout table with several calculators and plenty of bags. Bagging is a great job for young helpers.
- Have plenty of change on hand, and keep it in a belt pack, not on the table. Include stickers and a pen for markdowns at the end of the day. They're expected.
- Lock your house.
- Arrange for a charitable organization to pick up unsold items.
- Be ready early! Enthusiastically greet customers, be willing to negotiate, and have fun!

Lightening Your Load

As you sort, set aside items that you don't need but that might be useful to someone else. Moving sales add extra cash, but they also take time, especially to clean and price merchandise. If you decide to hold a sale, include a "kids' stuff only" section. Children may be more enthusiastic about sorting if they know they can keep the profits from selling.

You can sell items through consignment shops without the work of a sale. Consignment stores are springing up in every category, from clothing and exercise equipment to games and computers.

Charitable organizations—such as Disabled American Veterans, Goodwill, or Salvation Army—are a socially conscious alternative to a sale. Donating your excess or repairable appliances, furniture, clothes, and linens can help provide training and jobs, low-cost clothing, and household goods for the disadvantaged—plus the gift of time for you when you need it the most. Some organizations pick up large groups of items, and you may qualify for a tax deduction as large as what you might earn at a tag sale. Make a list of everything you donate so you won't have to rely on your memory at tax time.

Make a donation now and another after you pack. As you sort you will gain momentum and become more discriminating about what you keep. Chances are you'll run across things during packing that you have no idea why you kept.

Step Three: Packing—or *Not* Packing

If a moving company will be packing for you, this step will be easy—just select the items you want to pack yourself and things you want to take with you, including valuables and important documents and papers.

A cost-effective alternative to a moving company is to pack most items yourself, leaving the larger, more unwieldy accessories—artwork, mirrors, lamps, and electronic equipment to the pros. They have the right equipment and packing materials, and the cost may be only slightly more than renting or buying larger boxes and moving blankets. The cost of movers will usually be balanced by their efficiency in moving boxes and furniture with handcarts and straps especially designed for the purpose.

If you are moving partially or entirely yourself, start packing as soon as you've completed sorting every room. Purchase several sizes of sturdy moving boxes to get you started. I prefer to purchase boxes from a do-it-yourself moving company rather than gathering an assortment of boxes from stores. Although the cost is higher, the sizes are more efficient, which keeps the number of boxes to a minimum; you can purchase the quantity you need; and the boxes come knocked down to fit easily into a car, eliminating multiple trips to find and load bulky boxes. If you have friends who are moving, coordinate sharing boxes. During our last move three families moved within months of one another. We all shared boxes—and the cost!

Most move-it-yourself rental companies can help you determine how many boxes you'll need. However, estimate that a two-bedroom house will require 45 to 50 boxes, a three-bedroom 60 to 70 boxes, and a four-bedroom will need up to 100. Start with an assortment of sizes and about half the number of boxes you calculate you'll ultimately fill. Go back for more boxes when you have a better idea of what sizes you need. Unused and unassembled boxes can usually be returned.

When picking up boxes, be sure to include packing paper from

Moving with the Pros

If you will be using professional movers, start contacting companies as soon as you know your moving date. Call at least three companies, get references, and check them out. The Interstate Commerce Commission (ICC) regulates interstate moves, and cities and states will have guidelines and policies for local moves. In order to receive comparable estimates, make sure you provide each company with the same information. When estimators come to your house, show each the same rooms and household goods. Consider the following when making your choice:

✓ Additional charges. Local moves are usually priced hourly, and interstate moves are based on weight. Each will have additional charges for packing or unpacking, disconnecting (and connecting) appliances, large items such as pianos, and the number of stairs in your house.

✓ Discounts. Ask if you can obtain a discount for flexibility in loading and/or unloading dates.

✓ Binding or nonbinding estimate. If you know exactly what will be shipped, a binding estimate will provide a final cost. Although you may pay more for this type of estimate, you'll have a firm cost. With a nonbinding estimate, you'll pay an additional percentage (most companies have a 10 percent cap) if the cost of the move exceeds the estimate. Choose this option if you aren't certain what you'll be shipping.

✓ Mover's liability. Add extra insurance if your goods are valuable. Check your homeowner's policy to see if your goods are covered during transit.

On moving day be sure to read the bill of lading before signing and make certain all your items are listed. Take the bill of lading with you. You'll need it when the movers arrive and if you have to file any claims.

a do-it-yourself moving company or paper warehouse. Use it instead of newspaper to keep everything cleaner—including your hands. Use a packing tape dispenser for quick box assembly and sealing.

Before you start assemble a packing kit. Use your cleaning tote, and include the following items:

- ☐ Packing tape and dispenser
- ☐ Packing paper
- ☐ Utility knife
- ☐ Roll of red tape
- ☐ Paper towels
- ☐ Glass cleaner and all-purpose cleaner
- ☐ Scissors
- ☐ Box labels
- ☐ Marker
- ☐ Hammer
- ☐ Screwdrivers and pliers
- ☐ Zipper-lock plastic bags
- ☐ Self-adhesive file folder labels to mark small bagged items
- ☐ Small notebook and pen, or laptop computer, to record an inventory of each carton

Making It Stick

As you pack label each box with the main contents and the room in your new house where it should be delivered. Color-code labels according to rooms. The label in Appendix II is designed to wrap around the edge of the box for easy identification even when boxes are stacked. You can create labels on your computer, printing a different color for each room, or achieve the same result by adding a colored band with a highlighter to the end of any label. Round, self-adhesive, colored labels (three quarters of an inch or larger) will also work to eas-ily identify boxes by room (cover each label with a small piece of clear packing tape). If you don't write directly on the box, you'll be able to cover or remove the label and use the carton again without any confusion as to the contents.

Create FRAGILE labels to ease your mind about breakables and OPEN FIRST labels to keep you from having to open every box to locate what you need right away in your new home. Or run a length of red tape around the tops of boxes containing essentials. Help younger children pack an OPEN FIRST box for themselves. This activ-ity involves them in the process and provides the comfort of favorite things on the first night.

Deciding Where to Start

Begin packing those items you know you won't need for the next few weeks. Pack as much as you can now. If you aren't sure whether you'll need an item, pack it. Chances are you'll find a way to do without it.

✓ Use larger boxes for lighter items and smaller boxes for heavy things, like books. Keep packed weight to forty pounds or less.

✓ Pack light clothing in dresser drawers.

✓ Pack computers and electronic equipment in original cartons whenever possible. If you don't have the cartons, have your movers pack it, or wrap the equipment in plastic and purchase a sturdy box. Use padding (sweaters and blankets work well), and mark it FRAGILE.

✓ Put small parts in zipper-lock plastic bags. Label each bag by sticking a file folder label on the *inside.* Tape bags with related screws and bolts to the undersides of furniture.

As you finish with a room, stack boxes in the garage or another convenient place for easy loading on moving day.

Plan to pack in two stages: once when you finish sorting and a final stage just before the move. Spreading it out reduces the magnitude of the task. I usually underestimate how much time packing requires and am always delighted that I have done most of it ahead of time. After you've completed the first round, take a break and relax.

Watching All the Signs

Throughout the move pay close attention to the emotional needs of everyone in your household, especially children. When the tension mounts, recognize the important role your current house has played in your lives. It's been home. It's brought you together with friends who may soon be far away. Be prepared for some sadness to be mixed with the excitement, and take time to "let go" of the house. Here are some suggestions to ease the transition and add more fun and adventure to the process:

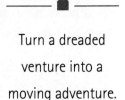

Turn a dreaded venture into a moving adventure.

- Have each family member choose a favorite place or activity in your town or neighborhood—the amusement park, a favorite golf course, museum, or the zoo. Schedule trips to break up the move, and bring a camera to record the memories.
- Make a home movie. If you don't have a video camera, rent or borrow one and let a child be the producer, walking through each room and recording memories. He or she can interview family members and neighbors. Our home movie included a section on neighborhood dogs!
- Make moving announcement cards. Take a photo of your family in front of your new house, and have reprints made. Purchase postcard backers (available at photo processing stores) and create personal "we've moved" cards. Address the postcards now and have them ready to drop in the mail when you arrive at your new house. If your new house is too far away to take the photo now, take a "moving in" photo when you arrive at your

new house. You'll have a perfect reason to take a few minutes out of a busy day to locate the nearest photo lab.

- Schedule a neighborhood farewell party. We held a potluck hors d'oeuvres open house for our neighbors two weeks before our move. It was an evening full of memories, and before it was over we made specific dates for get-togethers in our new house. Ask each person to bring a photo, make a scrapbook at the party, and have your friends sign it.

- Start a moving journal. Create a family journal or have each child make their own.
  - ✓ Purchase a small scrapbook or make your own with construction paper. Decorate the cover with markers and a photo of your current house.
  - ✓ Purchase a disposable camera, and encourage children to take photos of their friends and neighbors. Get autographs, and be sure to write addresses and phone numbers next to each picture. Take some photos yourself that include your children with their friends.
  - ✓ Include a photo of each child's room now.
  - ✓ Using graph paper, have children draw how they want to arrange and decorate their *new* rooms.
  - ✓ Help children write about people and things they will miss, and what is exciting—or scary—about the move.
  - ✓ Include pages to write and draw pictures about the move.

- Make "keep in touch" business cards for children to give to friends. (See Appendix II.) Make some for yourself, too, with laser-printer business cards available at office supply stores.

- Create a house poster for a child's new room. Include pictures of your old house and neighborhood, and leave room to add pictures of your new house and neighborhood. Use the format in Appendix II or create your own.

This End Up! Checklist

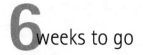

6 weeks to go

Organizing and Scheduling

- ☐ Hold a household meeting to discuss the move, and have everyone select jobs.
- ☐ Schedule sorting, room by room, over the next two weeks.
- ☐ Schedule good-byes for family, friends, children—lunches, an open house, coffee dates.
- ☐ Start a receipt envelope for moving expenses. Ask your accountant what expenses will be deductible so you won't have to reconstruct your expenditures at tax time.
- ☐ List all accounts and subscriptions requiring change of address notifications. Create a form letter on your computer.
- ☐ Make a list of items you have loaned to friends and neighbors.
- ☐ Start using perishables from your freezer.
- ☐ _____
- ☐ _____
- ☐ _____

Calls

- ☐ If you're a renter, notify your landlord. Review your lease to make sure you have complied with all deadlines and responsibilities.
- ☐ Request your free change of address kit from your postal carrier.
- ☐ Arrange for forwarding of W-2s and other tax forms.
- ☐ Arrange to transfer school records.

- [ ] Gather family dental and medical records, and other important papers. Have them sent ahead or take them with you.
- [ ] Schedule a cleaning service for moving day.
- [ ] Contact painters and decorators to schedule work before moving into your new house.

- [ ] _____
- [ ] _____
- [ ] _____

Sorting and Cleaning

- [ ] Select a gathering place for boxes of items to be sold or donated.
- [ ] Begin sorting.

- [ ] _____
- [ ] _____
- [ ] _____

Packing—Or Not

If You're Moving Yourself:

- [ ] Reserve a truck, movers, and accessories: dollies, padding, et cetera.

If You're Hiring a Moving Company:

- [ ] Select three movers and schedule estimates.

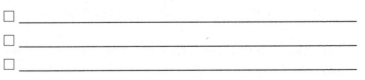

- [ ] _____
- [ ] _____
- [ ] _____

Errands and Notes

☐ Return items you have borrowed. Retrieve things on loan.

☐ _____

☐ _____

☐ _____

If You're Having a Sale:

☐ Plan the date.

☐ Set a cleaning and pricing schedule and enter it on your calendar.

☐ _____

☐ _____

☐ _____

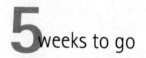

5 weeks to go

Organizing and Scheduling

☐ Send or fax change of address notices to accounts and subscriptions.

☐ Update your address list. Put it on your computer and create labels to save time when sending your postcards.

☐ Start a moving journal or scrapbook.

☐ Plan your home movie.

☐ _____

☐ _____

☐ _____

Calls

- ☐ Call your insurance agent, and check coverage on your possessions during the move.
- ☐ Reserve the elevator for moving out of or into a condo.
- ☐ Transfer your memberships: church, organizations, clubs.
- ☐ Check how to change your driver's license and license plates, if necessary.
- ☐ Talk with your vet about moving pets. Make necessary arrangements. Get a health and rabies vaccination certificate.

- ☐ _____
- ☐ _____
- ☐ _____

Sorting and Cleaning

- ☐ Continue sorting, room by room.
- ☐ Start memory boxes.

- ☐ _____
- ☐ _____
- ☐ _____

Packing—Or Not

If You're Moving Yourself:

- ☐ Gather or purchase moving boxes and packing paper.

- ☐ _____
- ☐ _____
- ☐ _____

Errands and Notes

☐ Purchase postcards for your moving announcements. Address them.

☐ _____

☐ _____

☐ _____

If You're Having a Sale:

☐ Write your ad.

☐ Print flyers.

☐ Rent tables.

☐ Make or order signs.

☐ Begin pricing and cleaning items.

☐ _____

☐ _____

☐ _____

4 weeks to go

Organizing and Scheduling

☐ Set dates for farewell parties. Call guests or design postcard invitations on your computer.

☐ _____

☐ _____

☐ _____

Calls

- ☐ Make arrangements for charity pickup of items to be donated.
- ☐ Register children in their new school.
- ☐ If you have a car loan, get permission from your financial institution to move it.
- ☐ Make travel and hotel arrangements, if necessary.
- ☐ Notify utility companies at both old and new addresses. Use the checklist on the facing page. Keep your telephone connected through moving day.

- ☐ _____
- ☐ _____
- ☐ _____

Sorting and Cleaning

- ☐ Finish sorting and start a thorough cleaning.

- ☐ _____
- ☐ _____
- ☐ _____

Packing—Or Not

If You're Moving Yourself:

- ☐ Create a packing kit.
- ☐ Begin packing, room by room.

- ☐ _____
- ☐ _____
- ☐ _____

Utilities

	Phone Number of Current Service	Phone Number of New Service
Gas	_____	_____
Electric	_____	_____
Water	_____	_____
Telephone	_____	_____
Cable TV	_____	_____
Water softener	_____	_____
Trash collection	_____	_____
Recycling collection	_____	_____
Newspaper	_____	_____
Security	_____	_____
Gardener	_____	_____
Pool service	_____	_____
_____	_____	_____
_____	_____	_____
_____	_____	_____

Errands and Notes

☐ _____

☐ _____

☐ _____

☐ _____

☐ _____

☐ _____

If You're Having a Sale:
- ☐ Continue to clean and price items.
- ☐ Place your ad.
- ☐ Distribute flyers to stores and neighbors.
- ☐ Pick up paper bags, flags, and balloons.
- ☐ Pick up T-shirts and visors for workers.
- ☐ Get change. Make sure you have a belt pack.
- ☐ Order box lunches, refreshments.

- ☐ _____
- ☐ _____
- ☐ _____

2 to 3 weeks to go

Be flexible in scheduling during the three weeks before a move. Allow time for changes and unexpected opportunities to spend time with friends and neighbors.

Organizing and Scheduling
- ☐ Host a farewell party for your children.
- ☐ Host your own good-bye party. Keep it simple.

- ☐ _____
- ☐ _____
- ☐ _____

Calls

- ☐ Cancel/change deliveries and services: newspapers, trash, et cetera.
- ☐ Select a new bank if you're moving out of the area. Ask your banker for a referral.
- ☐ Arrange for servicing of your appliances, if necessary.
- ☐ _____
- ☐ _____
- ☐ _____

Sorting and Cleaning

- ☐ _____
- ☐ _____
- ☐ _____

Packing—Or Not

If You're Moving Yourself:
- ☐ Continue packing, room by room.

If You're Hiring a Moving Company:
- ☐ Select and pack the items to take with you.
- ☐ _____
- ☐ _____
- ☐ _____

Errands and Notes

- ☐ Have your car serviced.
- ☐ Drain gas-powered equipment and take gas and oil to a collection site.
- ☐ Prune potted plants you want to move, take others to friends or place them in your sale.

☐ Return library books.
☐ Purchase items for an "essentials" box:
  ✓ Toilet paper
  ✓ Paper towels and spray cleaner
  ✓ Hand soap and dish soap
  ✓ Lightbulbs
  ✓ Snacks
  ✓ Paper plates
  ✓ Trash bags

☐ _____
☐ _____
☐ _____
☐ _____
☐ _____

If You're Having a Sale:
☐ Arrange tables and set up merchandise two days before sale day.
☐ Make a schedule for early-morning setup.
☐ Hold your sale.
☐ Go out for dinner (make a drop-off at the bank first).

☐ _____
☐ _____
☐ _____

1 week to go

Organizing and Scheduling

☐ _____
☐ _____
☐ _____
☐ _____
☐ _____

Calls

☐ Close your checking and savings accounts. Have the funds transferred to your new bank.

☐ _____
☐ _____
☐ _____
☐ _____
☐ _____

Sorting and Cleaning

☐ Clean appliances.
☐ Empty refrigerator and freezer 24 hours before moving day.

☐ _____
☐ _____
☐ _____
☐ _____

Packing—Or Not

If You're Moving Yourself:

☐ Finish packing your "essentials box" and label it OPEN FIRST or put red tape around the top for easy identification.

☐ Finish packing, leaving only the absolute necessities to be packed on moving day.

☐ Pack your telephone book! It'll come in handy for addresses and professional contacts.

If You're Hiring a Moving Company:

☐ Finish packing your "essentials box" and label it OPEN FIRST or put red tape around the top for easy identification.

☐ Set aside boxes you want to move yourself and mark them clearly so they don't get loaded accidentally.

☐ Contact your moving company and confirm their arrival time.

☐ Make a sketch of your new floor plan to help movers place boxes and furniture in the right rooms.

☐ _____

☐ _____

☐ _____

Errands and Notes

☐ Pick up traveler's checks or cash.

☐ Pick up dry cleaning and laundry.

☐ Close your safety-deposit box and place valuables in a safe place until you move.

☐ _____

☐ _____

☐ _____

MOVING DAY

- ☐ Take time with your family to walk through your house and say good-bye.
- ☐ Go through closets, basement, garage, et cetera, to make sure nothing is left behind.
- ☐ Turn off all lights, close and lock all windows and doors. Leave house keys with your real estate professional or new owners.
- ☐ Leave your new address and a phone number with the new owners so they can forward any mail missed by the post office.
- ☐ Make reservations for dinner or order carryout. It's time to treat yourself—you've made it through knowing which end's up!

If You're Moving Yourself:
- ☐ Pick up the truck early.
- ☐ Place your OPEN FIRST boxes on the truck last.

If You're Hiring a Moving Company:
- ☐ Ask your movers to place your OPEN FIRST boxes on the truck last.
- ☐ Read your bill of lading and verify the movers' final inventory of your belongings.
- ☐ Make sure the van driver has the exact address of your new home.
- ☐ Don't leave home until the truck is on its way.
- ☐ Designate someone to direct movers to put boxes in the correct room.

Telephone Numbers

Name   **Phone Number**

Real Estate Agent:

_____   _____

Mortgage Lenders:

_____   _____

_____   _____

Home Inspectors:

_____   _____

_____   _____

Real Estate Attorney:

_____   _____

Insurance Agent:

_____   _____

Tax Adviser:

_____   _____

School: _____   _____

Dentist: _____   _____

Doctor: _____   _____

Painters/Decorators:

_____   _____

_____   _____

Movers:

_____   _____

_____   _____

Memberships:

_____   _____

_____   _____

Bank: _____   _____

CHAPTER 8

Settling In

Most of my moves have been triggered by life events: marriage, job transfer, divorce, blending families. But only one move was strictly for the purpose of living in a larger house —nearly twice the size of our former house. The sense of space was invigorating. I reveled in empty cupboards when everything was unpacked. I was thrilled to discover a small closet under the stairs (the perfect size for storing table leaves!), an extra closet in an upstairs hall, and built-in drawers tucked away in bedroom closets. I was inspired by bookshelves with room for art, vases, and photos.

However, it's not so exhilarating moving to a smaller house or, like our last move, to one built on a smaller scale. Although the house was the same size in square footage, the details and room sizes were finer. It created a curious perception of loss of space that took some time to understand. Moving in was complicated at best.

We had most of our boxes moved before moving day, and both the dining room and den were filled with boxes labeled KITCHEN, leaving little room for furniture. Not a problem, I thought. We'll just unpack the kitchen boxes first to clear the space for furniture. However, the cleaning service hired by the former owners had misscheduled, and the kitchen was so dirty I didn't feel comfortable unpacking and putting away clean dishes and cooking utensils. So when the moving van arrived, the dining room and den were full, and the furnishings were placed in the living room—already overpowered by large furniture and overrun by boxes!

To further complicate matters, our queen-size mattresses didn't fit up the narrow hallway to the second floor. The movers passed mattresses brigade style from the front stairs to the roof of the porch, and onto the third-floor sundeck before bringing them inside. Once inside the mattresses had to be maneuvered back to the second floor by cutting a hole in a newly remodeled hallway wall. Needless to say, moving in took longer than we'd anticipated. As the movers approached overtime, I began to look for ways to speed the process. I directed every box to the sunroom, the only area with any open space.

When we were left alone, I was disheartened by the apparent lack of space. I felt we'd purchased a home too small for our furniture and possessions.

That evening my brother, who has moved more times than anyone can count, called to ask if we needed help. When I replied that we were "just fine," he heard the discouragement in my voice and said, "I'll be right over." He walked in, looked around, and said, "Whoa! The first thing we do is order a pizza. The second thing we do is arrange one room so you can think clearly." He started moving boxes out of the living room and arranging furniture. He found the lamps and hooked up the stereo. Within an hour we were relaxing in the living room and talking about what furniture to keep and what we wanted to replace.

It was all we needed to get past the overwhelming feeling of boxes everywhere and to make a plan for the next day. On the first morning in our new house, we had coffee in the living room, leisurely read the newspaper, and went out for breakfast before we touched a box!

Regardless of how many times you've moved, how many possessions you've accumulated, or how organized your preparations, when the movers leave it feels like order will never reign again. You've spent weeks organizing details, uncluttering your life, boxing up possessions, and clearing out rooms. Then, in a few short hours, all your hard work seems to unravel before your eyes. It's easy to become overwhelmed by the boxes and the feeling of disorder. Add a new neighborhood, new routine, and family members who need attention, and you've got the makings of chaos.

Getting settled involves more than unpacking. You and your household are in transition from comfortable surroundings to unfamiliar territory. Little details or unexpected problems are easily magnified. Having a plan to fall back on will help minimize these problems and provide a foundation for establishing new rhythms and routines as quickly and smoothly as possible. Integrating the emotional needs of a household in transition will build a sense of unity and accomplishment.

Moving Day

When you arrive at your new house, start with the fundamentals. Check pilot lights for water heater, appliances, and furnace. Make sure all utilities have been hooked up.

Getting enough rest and maintaining routines will play a key role in how you and your household handle the next few weeks. Set up beds and children's rooms first. Getting children settled in their rooms will help them reach a comfort level sooner in their new environment. When the beds are made and your OPEN FIRST boxes are unpacked, set the stage for the next few days and weeks.

Create a haven—a family room or living room can quickly become a refuge from boxes and paper and provide space for conversation and relaxation. You don't need every accessory in place to establish a feeling of comfort. Arrange furniture with the understanding that you'll probably rearrange it later. Add a television, VCR, and CD player for instant relaxation. Pick up a bouquet of flowers on your first errand to make this room feel like home. Keep a basket of fresh fruit and snacks available for your household and any guests who couldn't wait for the first invitation.

To ease the chaos, make one room home.

Smooth the way with familiarity. As the first few days in your new home speed by, try to maintain some everyday routines—enjoy meals together and discuss what's happening. Take time out to rent a movie. Go for a walk through the neighborhood, and help your children meet new friends. Explore, and familiarize yourself with your community: go to the supermarket and try several restaurants. Increase your exercise. You'll have more energy to unpack and organize your house when your day isn't filled with stress and tension.

Set Your Stage

Create a house that feels spacious, comfortable, and well cared for by following the basics of (1) cleaning, (2) organizing, and (3) repairing. Bringing order to rooms will bring a peacefulness to the house and everyone in it—and set the stage for the years to follow. You'll discover every little nook and cranny, have time to think about what you want to place where, and make a wish list of what's needed to make the space reflect your decorating and lifestyle.

Cleaning your entire house before you put everything away not only will provide a fresh environment but is an ideal way to really get to know your house and take ownership of the space. When it's freshly cleaned or painted, unpacking becomes more organized and efficient. You'll find every little repair item and be more likely to take care of it than if you hurriedly put everything away. Remember, everyday life itself will soon return, and you'll be more inclined to "make do" when your routine is back to normal.

Start a house journal. Use a notebook to make lists of items to purchase, repairs to be made, and ideas that come to you while you're cleaning, unpacking, and organizing your new space. A five-by-seven-inch spiral notebook with four or five sections is perfect. In the first section keep a master list of maintenance to be done and repairs to be made. Create smaller, daily (or weekend) lists to work from. Label separate sections in the notebook to record the specifics of maintenance and repairs, decorating projects, and gardening notes. It will be invaluable when you want to know exactly what color you painted a room, or who you called that did a great (or not so great) job fixing the sink or trimming the shrubs. Keep a separate folder for articles and ideas you want to save about home-related projects and decorating.

Create a blueprint for organized living.

These techniques—organizing, cleaning, repairing, neutralizing, and Dynamizing—were first introduced in my Dress Your House for Success concept, designed for preparing a home for sale. The most frequent comment from clients who use the program is, "My house looks and feels so great, I wish I'd done this five years ago!" It made me realize these are rules to live, not just sell, by. A friend recently followed all the steps and staged her small, 1,000-square-foot home to feel open and much larger. She cleaned every window and painted every surface—including the basement—white. She reduced furniture and accessories to a minimum, incorporating simple decorating techniques in scale with her home. The result: a house that felt comfortable and inviting from the moment you entered. This is a feeling that costs almost nothing to achieve. And the best time to do it is now.

Cleaning

It's ideal to be able to move into a house that is thoroughly clean; however, not all moving schedules are flexible enough to provide that luxury. Also, someone else's standards of cleanliness may not measure up to yours. A house that's clean is energizing. Whether you prefer to start in the kitchen, as I do, the bath, or somewhere in between, begin each room by cleaning every inch of space before you fill it. Pay special attention to light, and bring the sunshine into a room by cleaning windows and draperies. Clean and restore woodwork to make the room glow. When all the surfaces are clean, the light they reflect creates an ambience of warmth and comfort.

A house that's clean is energizing.

Now is a perfect time for a new rule if you have smokers in your household: Take it outside! Remind smokers that smoking indoors creates a film on everything—from windows and furniture to picture frames and knickknacks.

If a thorough cleaning fails to make things feel like new, put a new coat of paint on your list. In our last two homes we painted closets before storing clothes and linens. A closet takes only a few minutes to paint and will dry as you are cleaning other areas of the room. Put on a second coat, unpack, and the closet may already be dry. Or delegate closet detail to the painter in your household. He or she can be one room ahead of the unpacking. Use latex paint, and wrap brushes and rollers in plastic wrap between paintings to eliminate the chore of cleaning up.

If you don't like the color of a room or the green shag carpeting in the basement now, you won't like it any better next year. Make a list in your notebook of what you really don't like. When you're settled in, evaluate when to start making your house reflect your personal tastes.

Beware of the "it'll do" syndrome. If you find yourself thinking, It's good enough for now, I'll change it later, remember that very shortly your life will take over again. You won't see all the little details in your house, regardless of your housekeeping habits. You won't notice the closets that were left 1950s green or the woodwork that wasn't a priority to clean and polish. If you don't find the time for the fundamentals now, you might never find it. Use one section of your notebook for future projects, and schedule them over the next months as your time and budget allow.

Organizing

Moving in is the perfect time to make sure that every drawer, cupboard, and closet creates an organized feeling in your house. It's easy to just toss utensils in drawers or stack towels and linens haphazardly in a closet when you're in a rush to get on to the next box. Take a few extra minutes to create a feeling of organization that will send a subtle message of order every time a drawer or door is opened. Cabinet and drawer organizers are inexpensive and can extend the space when it all seems to be taken.

Stamp out clutter.

Facing, a merchandising technique you see every day in supermarkets and department stores, is accomplished by turning labels forward and stacking books, games, and puzzles flush, with larger ones on the bottom. An orderly arrangement of items on shelves will actually create more room. Trifold blankets, sheets, and towels in closets to accomplish the same look. If you don't cram cupboards, closets, and medicine cabinets full, your whole house will feel more spacious. Apply the same technique to the workroom, laundry room, and garage. Avoid the temptation to leave tools and other supplies in a box until you need them. Hang tools so they are easily accessible. Face paint cans, and label each with where and when it was used. Invest in organizers for your garage, too. When the space is organized, it's easier to undertake the chores you may otherwise put off.

As you unpack evaluate again if an item has outlived its usefulness, and gather articles for a final donation to charity. When you come across things you're not sure "fit," but you aren't sure you want to give away, set them aside rather than putting them away. After you're settled in you can reevaluate whether to use, store, or give them away.

Organize your furniture and accessories, too. Furniture that is too large or too much for the space can make a room—and an entire house—feel smaller than it is. The room arrangement basics that follow will help you plan how to open space and create uncluttered, comfortable rooms. Adding a mirror can increase the perception of size in a room and bring a further dimension of light. If your house has extra doors that remain open all the time, consider removing and storing them in the garage or attic to open space.

Repairing

As you move through your house cleaning and organizing, you'll undoubtedly come across little items in need of repair. Keep your notebook with you, and write down every item you want

Room Arrangement Basics

You can make any room feel larger when you place the furniture so as to create a sense of space. Follow these basics, then add accessories to personalize it and make it feel comfortable.

✓ Place large pieces of furniture on opposite ends of the room and away from doors for an uncluttered entrance.

✓ Avoid competing focal points on one wall. For example, placing a large entertainment center on the same wall as a fireplace adds a second focal point and creates a visual imbalance.

✓ Match the scale of the furniture with the space it occupies: small pieces on large walls will feel lost; large pieces will overpower small spaces.

✓ Place sofas and chairs eight to ten inches away from walls, and angle chairs or tables so the room doesn't look stiff and uninviting.

✓ Create a conversation area: Flank a fireplace or love seat with two chairs for cozy chats. Add an area rug to define the space.

✓ Arrange a bookcase to display art and photos, too.

✓ Group accessories in threes: a vase filled with flowers, a decorative bowl, and a stack of books on a table will be interesting without creating the feeling of clutter.

✓ Not all pictures and artwork must be hung. Photos placed on the floor, a plate, or a gallery ledge add interest.

to fix or replace. From cracked switch plates to torn screens, you'll see it all when you're cleaning and unpacking.

A house in good repair feels well cared for, and maintaining your home's good condition will add to its value. When you're settled in, divide your repair list into manageable, affordable segments. You'll have a house in tip-top shape in no time.

Take a Break

When the last box is unpacked, it's time to let everything settle. Live in your house for several months, even a year, before embarking on major remodeling projects or furniture purchases. Try your furniture and accessories in different rooms. You may be surprised by how well your furnishings work in your new space. It takes time to know a house, including how individual areas and rooms support different activities. You'll make wiser decisions when you have the benefit of time and familiarity.

Use these next few months instead to strengthen roots in your new community. Starting fresh is an exciting and rare opportunity. Make the most of it by devising a plan to participate in activities and groups with interests similar to your own. You'll be sure to meet people with whom you'll have something in common—and that's guaranteed to help you grow new roots.

✔ Join a group. Look into the local PTA, theater group, women's clubs, environmental organizations, political organizations, gardening club, walking group, et cetera.

✔ Volunteer. Help at your child's school. Or look into a cultural or charitable organization that might need your expertise. If art is your passion, contact museums. Look in your newspaper for volunteer listings or contact the Chamber of Commerce for groups whose missions fit your interests.

✓ Join a community sports team. Your kids will meet children their own age, and there's nothing like a rousing Little League game to foster friendships among parents. If your family doesn't include children, consider volunteering. You'll meet new neighbors of all ages and get to know the workings of your community.

Common interests establish new roots.

✓ Join an old group. Look into organizations you belonged to before that might have chapters in your new area, such as political organizations, college alumni groups, or emergency relief volunteers. Reciprocal memberships in clubs and museums will provide a common ground to build new friendships.

Coming Home

You're home. You've stopped along the way to experience the excitement and trepidation of everything a move encompasses—searching for the *right* house in the *right* neighborhood, waiting for the news that it's yours, and organizing all the details necessary to relocate a household with its

roots intact. You've accomplished the basic steps of settling in. You're on your way to creating a space that will build on that magical feeling of coming home. When you think about it, that's what you've been striving for throughout this process: a place of comfort and refuge from the hustle and stress of daily living—a space that embraces you and renews your spirit every time it welcomes you home.

Appendix I: Property Information Sheet*

Date:_____

Property address: _____

_____

_____

Seller(s): _____

Telephone: _____

The Seller(s) states that the information in this disclosure is correct to the best of the Seller's current actual knowledge as of the above date. This is not a warranty of any kind by the Seller(s).

When was the house built? _____

When did you purchase the house? _____

Foundation

Are there cracks, mildew, leaks, or dampness in the floor or in the foundation walls? ☐ Yes ☐ No
Explain: _____

_____

Has there been any previous water seepage in the basement, crawl space, foundation walls, or foundation slab? ☐ Yes ☐ No
Explain: _____

_____

Have there been any repairs to the foundation? ☐ Yes ☐ No
Explain: _____

_____

Is there any evidence of rodents, powder-post beetles, termites, carpenter ants, or any other insect infestation? ☐ Yes ☐ No

*This material is courtesy of Stein + Stein Relocation Management; used by permission.

Explain: _____

_____

Has there been any previous infestation that has been treated or
repaired?   ☐ Yes ☐ No
Explain: _____

_____

Are there any warranties in effect in connection with the treatment
for infestation?   ☐ Yes (Please attach copies.) ☐ No
Is the property located on filled or expansive soil?   ☐ Yes ☐ No
Explain: _____

_____

Are you aware of any sliding, settling, earth movement, upheavals, or
earth stability problems that have occurred on your property or in
the immediate neighborhood?   ☐ Yes ☐ No
Explain: _____

_____

Are you aware of any other defects or problems relating to the foundation or basement?   ☐ Yes ☐ No
Explain: _____

_____

Roof

What is the age of the present roof? _____
Has the roof been repaired for any reason?   ☐ Yes ☐ No
Explain: _____

_____

Has there been any evidence of leaks, storm damage, or gutter
backup?   ☐ Yes ☐ No
Explain: _____

_____

Are there any warranties on the roof?
                              ☐ Yes (Please attach copies.) ☐ No

Heating and Cooling

What type of heating does the house have (gas, coal, wood, electric,
   propane, etc.)? _____

Has the service been adequate?   ☐ Yes ☐ No

What type of air-conditioning system does the house have?

_____

Has the service been adequate?   ☐ Yes ☐ No

Are you aware of any problems affecting the heating
   system?   ☐ Yes ☐ No
   Explain: _____

_____

Are you aware of any problems affecting the air-conditioning
   system?   ☐ Yes ☐ No
   Explain: _____

_____

Electrical

What type of wiring does the house have (copper, aluminum, BX,
   Romex)? _____

What amp service? _____ Fuses or circuit breakers? _____

Are you aware of any problems affecting the electrical
   system?   ☐ Yes ☐ No
   Explain: _____

_____

Has the electrical service or system been updated?   ☐ Yes ☐ No
   When? _____
   By whom? _____

Plumbing

What type of plumbing does the house have (copper, lead, cast iron, PVC, etc.)?_____

Explain: _____

_____

Are you aware of any problems affecting the plumbing
system?   ☐ Yes ☐ No

Explain: _____

_____

Has the plumbing been updated?   ☐ Yes ☐ No

When? _____

By whom? _____

Water

What is the house's source of drinking water (municipal, well,
etc.)? _____

If it is a private source, when was it last tested? (date)_____

Have there been any water tests (coliform, nitrate) that were unsatis-
factory?   ☐ Yes ☐ No

Explain: _____

_____

Are there any wells on the property?   ☐ Yes ☐ No

If so, how many?_____

Is the well in use?   ☐ Yes ☐ No

If not, has it been sealed?   ☐ Yes ☐ No

Sewage

What type of sewage system does the house have (municipal or
septic)? _____

Is the property connected to a public sewer system?   ☐ Yes ☐ No

Has there been any sewage backup?   ☐ Yes ☐ No

   Explain: _____

_____

When was the last septic inspection? (date)_____

When was the last septic cleanout? (date) _____

Is the septic system within the lot lines?   ☐ Yes ☐ No

   Explain: _____

_____

Watering System

Are there in-ground sprinklers?   ☐ Yes ☐ No

Irrigation?   ☐ Yes ☐ No

Is the watering system in operating condition?   ☐ Yes ☐ No

Pool/Spa

Is there a pool?   ☐ Yes ☐ No

Is it in-ground or aboveground? _____

What type and size pool is it (preformed, vinyl liner, gunite, tile)?____

   Explain: _____

_____

What pool equipment is included in the sale of the

   property? _____

    Are the pool and equipment in good operating

      condition?   ☐ Yes ☐ No

Is there a spa?   ☐ Yes ☐ No

   Is it in good operating condition?   ☐ Yes ☐ No

Land and Site

Do any of the following exist?

	Yes	No		Yes	No
Easements	☐	☐	Lead paint	☐	☐
Encroachments	☐	☐	Asbestos	☐	☐
Boundary disputes	☐	☐	Radon gas	☐	☐
Zoning violations	☐	☐	Ureaformaldehyde	☐	☐
Soil problems	☐	☐	Insulation	☐	☐
Diseased trees	☐	☐	Underground	☐	☐
Standing water	☐	☐	Fuel tank	☐	☐
Floodplain	☐	☐			

Explain: _____

_____

Have you ever experienced problems (interior or exterior) with ground-
water runoff after heavy rains or spring thaws? ☐ Yes ☐ No
Explain: _____

_____

Has the property had drainage or flooding problems? ☐ Yes ☐ No
Explain: _____

_____

Does the property share a private driveway with another
property? ☐ Yes ☐ No
Explain: _____

_____

Are there any past or present problems with driveways, walkways,
patio, seawalls, fences, retaining walls, or party walls on the
property or adjacent properties? ☐ Yes ☐ No
Explain: _____

_____

Have there ever been problems with roots growing into foundations
or sewer pipes? ☐ Yes ☐ No
Explain: _____

Is the property located on an earthquake fault? ☐ Yes ☐ No

Are there any other known defects in or on the

property? ☐ Yes ☐ No

Explain: _____

_____

Have you or previous owners made any structural additions, changes,

or repairs to the property without obtaining all necessary permits

and government approvals? ☐ Yes ☐ No

Explain: _____

_____

Are you aware of any threatened or legal action affecting this

property? ☐ Yes ☐ No

Explain: _____

_____

Other

Have the following ever occurred?

Fire? ☐ Yes ☐ No

Date:_____Location: _____

Explain: _____

_____

Flooding? ☐ Yes ☐ No

Date:_____Location: _____

Explain: _____

_____

Plumbing freeze-up? ☐ Yes ☐ No

Date:_____Location: _____

Explain: _____

_____

Assessments

Are there any unpaid assessments? ☐ Yes ☐ No
   Explain: _____

_____

Do you have notice of any future assessments? ☐ Yes ☐ No
   Explain: _____

_____

Neighborhood

Does an unusual amount of noise from any one source (for example,
   airplanes, motorized vehicles, schools, or businesses) affect the
   property? ☐ Yes ☐ No
   Explain: _____

_____

Have you encountered problems with noisy residents, or have animals
   caused disturbances? ☐ Yes ☐ No
   Explain: _____

_____

General Condition

Do you know of any other facts, conditions, or circumstances that
   may affect the value, beneficial use, or desirability of this
   property? ☐ Yes ☐ No
   Explain: _____

_____

The above information is true and correct to the best of my (our)
   knowledge.

Seller: _____ Date: _____

Seller: _____ Date: _____

Appendix II: Moving Materials

Open This Box
FIRST

MEMORY BOX

Name _____

Contents _____

_____

_____

_____

_____

Room: _Kitchen_____

Contents:_____

_____

_____

_____

THIS END UP
A moving survival kit

KITCHEN

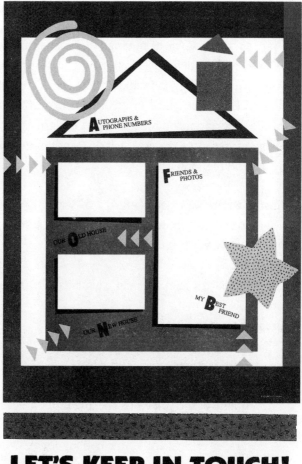

LET'S KEEP IN TOUCH!

My new address:

My new phone number:

Signed:

Appendix III: Words, Terms, and Real Estate

During the course of buying your home, many terms will be used with which you may or may not be familiar. The most common terminology is included here; however, if you are unfamiliar with any language in a contract or during a conversation regarding an option or process, ask for clarification. Questioning one of your resource professionals is a mark of thoroughness rather than a sign of ignorance.

Adjustable Rate Mortgage (ARM)
A mortgage that allows the interest rate to adjust up or down periodically, relative to a financial index.

Amortization
Repayment of a loan in equal payments of principal and interest.

Annual Percentage Rate (APR)
The total finance charge, including interest, fees, and points, expressed as a percentage of the loan.

Appraisal
An estimate of the value of a specific property.

Assumption of Mortgage
A buyer's agreement to assume liability for an existing mortgage, subject to the lender's approval.

Binder
An acknowledgment of a deposit accompanying a written agreement to enter into a contract for the sale of real estate.

Broker
An individual who holds a real estate broker's license for a company or branch office. A broker may or may not work with customers.

Cap

The limit on how much the interest rate or monthly payment can change.

Closing

The meeting where ownership of a property is legally transferred from seller to buyer.

Comparative (Competitive) Market Analysis (CMA)

A report of features and selling prices of comparable houses on the market or recently sold used to develop a price for a house to be placed on the market.

Contingency

A condition that must be met before a contract is binding.

Contract

A legally binding agreement between two or more parties.

Conversion Clause

A clause in a mortgage that allows an ARM to be converted to a fixed rate loan after a specified period.

Down Payment

The percentage of the purchase price that must be paid in cash and not borrowed from the lender.

Earnest Money

The portion of the down payment made at the time of the purchase offer as a sign of good faith.

Equity

The portion of the property actually owned by the homeowner: original purchase price plus appreciation and improvements, less loans and liens.

Escrow

A procedure by which a third party assumes responsibility for paperwork and distribution of funds at the instruction of both buyer and seller.

FHA Mortgage

A loan insured by the Federal Housing Administration.

Fixed Rate Mortgage

A mortgage for which the interest rate remains the same over the life of the loan.

Home Inspection Report

A report made by a home inspector that evaluates the structural condition and mechanical systems of a property.

Home Warranty Plan

Protection against failure of a property's mechanical systems and appliances during the listing period and a specified period after closing.

Index

A measure of interest rate changes used to determine changes in an ARM's interest rate.

MLS (Multiple Listing Service)

A system that provides members detailed information about properties for sale.

Mortgage

A claim by a lender against a property until the loan or services have been paid.

Negative Amortization

When monthly payments do not cover interest costs, the interest is added to the principal balance. This could occur when an ARM has a payment cap, and you could end up owing more than you borrowed.

Origination Fee

The fee for processing a proposed mortgage loan.

PITI

Principal, interest, taxes, and insurance.

PMI (Private Mortgage Insurance)

Insurance that protects a lender against loss if a homeowner defaults on the mortgage.

Point

One percent of the loan principal.

Purchase Agreement

A written contract between a seller and purchaser of real estate property stating terms and conditions of the sale. Also referred to as a sales contract or earnest money contract.

Real Estate Agent

An individual who holds a license to sell real estate. He or she represents a buyer or seller in the buying or selling of property. A real estate agent must work for a licensed real estate broker or firm.

Realtor

A member of the National Association of Realtors.

Sales Contract

See Purchase Agreement.

Title

A document that is evidence of ownership of a specific property.

Title Insurance

A policy that protects against loss from legal defects in a property's title.

Title Search

A detailed check of title records to identify any legal encumbrances that affect a seller's right to sell.

VA Mortgage

A mortgage loan for qualified veterans guaranteed by the Veterans Administration.

Index

adjustable rate mortgage (ARM), 86, 184
  convertible, 87, 185
agency, dual, 78
agent(s), real estate, 47, 120, 131, 184
  buyer's vs. seller's, 78
  buying a home without assistance of, 76, 79–81
  choosing of, 80–81
  loyalty to, 78–79
  working with, 76–77, 109
amortization, 184
  negative, 186
annual percentage rate, 184
appraisal, 184
assumption of mortgage, 184

banks, 84
binder, 124, 184
broker, 185
business cards, 150
buying a home. *See* homebuying; purchasing a
  house

cap, 185
cards, business, 150
charitable donations, 144, 172
checklists:
  HomePrint Summary, 95
  moving, 151–64
children, 149, 150
  closing and, 132
  house tours and, 98, 110
  memory boxes and, 141
  moving day and, 167
  moving journals and, 150
  packing and, 35, 148
  schools for, 35, 46, 48
cleaning, when moving in, 169–71
cleaning and sorting, in moving, 139–44
  checklists for, 152, 154, 156, 159, 161
cleanliness of houses, in tours, 103–5
closing, 131–33, 185
closing date, 126
clutter, 102–3
community, 48, 49, 174–75
comparative (competitive) market analysis (CMA),
  185

compromising (settling), 16, 30–32, 54, 111
contingencies, 125–26, 185
contract, 120, 185. *See also* purchase agreement
convertible ARM, 87, 185

decorating styles, 107–8
deposit, earnest money (binder), 124, 184, 185
design features, 107–8
donations to charity, 144, 172
down payment, 65–67, 85, 185
  earnest money and, 124
dual agency, 78

emotions:
  buying a particular house based on, 30–32, 42,
    54–56
  closing and, 132–33
  moving and, 134–36, 141, 149
equity, 185
escrow, 186
extermination, 105

FHA mortgage, 87, 186
financial investment, 113–14
financing. *See* mortgage
fixed rate mortgage, 86, 186
floor plan, 58, 111
furniture, 111–12
  arrangement of, 172, 173

Game of Nines, 33–39
  HomePrint and, 33, 36, 43, 45, 59
garage sales, 142–43, 144
  checklists for, 153, 155, 158, 160
glossary of terms, 184–87

homebuying:
  emotions in. *See* emotions
  Game of Nines in, 33–39, 43, 45, 59
  HomePrint Summary, 95
  planning and defining stage of, 19. *See also*
    HomePrint
  purchase in. *See* purchasing a house
  selection process in, 19–20. *See also* houses,
    looking at
  settling (compromising) in, 16, 30–32, 54, 111

three stages of, 18–21
timing of, when selling a house, 93–94,
    125–26, 132
HomeFinders' Kit, 98
home inspection, 75, 90–92, 105, 130–31
    choosing an inspector for, 91
    contingency clause for, 125
    report in, 186
    see also pest inspection
home movies, 149
HomePrint, 40–72, 96, 102, 108, 111
    estimation of your buying power in, 42, 63–72
    Game of Nines and, 33, 36, 43, 45, 59
    location in. *See* location
    Summary, 95
    type of house in, 42, 54–62, 63
    worksheets for, 51–53, 59–62, 69–72
home warranty plan, 126, 186
Househunters' Notes, 102, 110, 115–18
house journal, 169, 170–71
house poster, 150
houses, looking at, 96–118
    avoiding confusion in, 109–10
    cleanliness and, 103–5
    clutter and, 102–3
    "curb appeal" and, 100–102
    and design features and decorating styles,
        107–8
    HomeFinders' Kit in, 98
    Househunters' Notes in, 102, 110, 115–18
    obtaining insights from houses you don't like,
        108–9
    repairs and remodeling and, 105–7, 113–14
    what to do when you think you've found the
        right house, 111–14

index, 186
inspection. *See* home inspection; pest inspection
insurance:
    homeowners', 92, 131
    mortgage, 66, 84, 131, 187
    mover's, 146
    title, 92–93, 187
interest rate, 88, 186
interest rate factor chart, 72
Internet, 81

journals:
    house, 169, 170–71
    moving, 150

labels, packing, 147–48
lead paint, 126–27
lists of likes and dislikes (Game of Nines), 33–39,
    43, 45, 59
loans:
    piggyback, 84–85
    see also mortgage
location, 41–42, 43–53, 63, 111
    confirming, 112–13
    evaluating, 46–47, 48–49

worksheet for, 51–53
looking at houses. *See* houses, looking at

memory boxes, 141
MLS (Multiple Listing Service), 77, 186
mortgage, 186
    adjustable rate, 86, 87, 184, 185
    applying for, 75, 85–88, 129–30
    biweekly payments on, 65
    choosing of, 86–87
    convertible, 87, 185
    delays in, 130
    documentation needed for, 88–89
    down payment and, 65–67, 85
    estimating your buying power, 42, 63–72
    FHA, 87, 186
    finalizing of, 128–30
    fixed rate, 86, 186
    insurance, 66, 84, 131, 187
    interest rate on, 88
    interest rate chart for, 72
    length of, 64
    piggyback loans and, 84–85
    preapproval of, 75, 82–83, 128, 129
    prequalification of, 83
    purchase agreement and, 125
    selecting a lender for, 84–85
    VA, 87, 187
mortgage bankers, 84
mortgage brokers, 84
movies, home, 149
moving, 134–64
    checklist for, 151–64
    emotions and, 134–36, 141, 149
    making journals, 150
    making memory boxes, 141
    organizing and scheduling in, 136–38
    organizing and scheduling checklists for,
        151–52, 153–54, 155–56, 158–59, 161
    packing in. *See* packing
    selling and donating possessions, 142–43, 144
    selling possessions, checklists for, 153, 155,
        158, 160
    sorting and cleaning in, 139–44
    sorting and cleaning checklists for, 152, 154,
        156, 159, 161
    suggestions for easing the transition and
        making it more fun, 149–50
moving announcement cards, 149–50
moving companies, 144, 145
    checklists for working with, 152, 159, 162, 163
    selection of, 146, 152
moving day, 167–68
    checklist for, 163
moving in, 165–75
    cleaning and, 169–71
    community and, 174–75
    moving day, 167–68
    organizing and, 171–72
    repairs and, 169, 172–74
    room arrangement and, 172, 173

moving process, 26–29
   children in. *See* children
   life changes and, 24–26, 27, 35
   see also homebuying; moving
Multiple Listing Service (MLS), 77, 186

negative amortization, 186
neighborhood farewell party, 150
neighborhood of new house, *see* location

offer, 120, 121–28. *See also* price; purchase
   agreement
organizing, after moving in, 171–72
organizing and scheduling, in moving, 136–38
   checklists for, 151–52, 153–54, 155–56,
     158–59, 161
origination fee, 186

packing, 144–49
   checklists for, 152, 154, 156, 159, 162
   children and, 35, 148
   kit, 147
   labels in, 147–48
   see also moving
paint, lead, 126–27
painting, 170
party, farewell, 150
personal property, in purchase agreement, 124–25
pest inspection, 105, 126
PITI, 187
point, 187
possession date, 126
poster, house, 150
price, 82
   asking (list) vs. selling, 67, 121
   bidding games and, 123
   and condition of property, 43, 122
   estimating your buying power, 42, 63–72
   and length of time on market, 93, 123
   making an offer, 120, 121–28
   and owners' reasons for selling, 122–23
   of similar houses, 121–22
private mortgage insurance (PMI), 66, 84, 131,
   187
professional resources, 73–93, 119–20
   agents. *See* agent(s), real estate
   home inspectors, 91. *See also* home inspection
   insurance agents, 92, 131. *See also* insurance
   lenders, 84–85. *See also* mortgage
   tax advisers, 85
property information sheet, 176–83
purchase agreement, 89–90, 112, 120, 124–28,
   130, 187
   terms and conditions in, 105, 124–27
purchasing a house, 20, 119–33
   "buyer's remorse" and, 129

closing in, 131–33
down payment in, 65–67, 85, 124
finalizing financing for, 128–30
home inspection in. *See* home inspection
insurance and, 131
making an offer, 120, 121–28
price in. *See* price
purchase agreement in. *See* purchase agreement
timing of, when selling another house, 93–94,
   125–26, 132
see also mortgage

real estate agent. *See* agent(s), real estate
real estate environment, 48, 113, 121
Realtor, 187
remodeling, 105–7, 113–14
repairs:
   looking at houses in need of, 105–7
   moving in and, 169, 172–74
   selling price and, 122
resources. *See* professional resources

sales contract. *See* purchase agreement
scheduling and organizing, in moving, 136–38
   checklists for, 151–52, 153–54, 155–56,
     158–59, 161
schools, 35, 46, 48
selling your house:
   contingency providing for, 125–26
   location and, 50
   remodeling and, 113–14
   timing of, when buying another, 93–94,
     125–26, 132
settling (compromising), 16, 30–32, 54, 111
settling in. *See* moving in
sorting and cleaning, in moving, 139–44
   checklists for, 152, 154, 156, 159, 161

tax laws, 29, 85
telephone numbers, 164
terminology, 184–87
title, 187
title insurance, 92–93, 187
title search, 187
type of house, 42, 54–62, 63
   worksheet for, 59–62

utilities checklist, 157

VA (Veterans Administration) mortgage, 87, 187

walkthrough, 126, 131–32
worksheets, HomePrint, 111
   estimating your buying power, 69–72
   location, 51–53
   type of house, 59–62